RECLAIMING VATICAN II

"The great missionary vision of Vatican II remains largely unrealized. This book shows how to recover it, primarily by returning to the council's four major constitutions. Fr. Blake Britton is an able guide, radiant and thoughtful, with an infectious joy and love for the council. He stands on the vanguard of a new generation tasked with finally bringing the council's vision to fruition. I warmly commend this book to anyone wanting to understand Vatican II, but especially to young Catholics confused about the council and those skeptical about its relevance today."

Most Rev. Robert Barron
Auxiliary Bishop of Los Angeles and
founder of Word on Fire Catholic Ministries

"Sixty years after the Second Vatican Council commenced, two extremes remain locked in battle: traditionalists scorn the council and want to dismiss it, claiming it's the root of the Church's biggest problems today; while liberals maintain the council didn't go far enough in its progressive reforms. Between those extremes, many faithful Catholics are just confused—unsure what to make of Vatican II. Was it good? Bad? Somewhere in between? Fr. Blake Britton, the most enthusiastic and insightful defender of the council among millennial Catholics, guides us through this confusion to show why the Second Vatican Council remains one of the Holy Spirit's greatest gifts to the Church. He explains why the council was needed, what the texts taught and intended, and how they were sadly misimplemented. More importantly, he shows how we can get the conciliar reforms back on track by returning to the texts themselves. We've desperately needed a book like this. It's timely, clear, charitable, inspiring, faithful to the Church, and strikes all the right notes. If every Catholic read this book and followed its path, liturgies would become more reverent, biblical studies would be renewed, the Church would be more confident about her identity, and evangelization would flourish—exactly what Vatican II had in mind!"

Brandon Vogt
Senior content director at Word on Fire Catholic Ministries
and author of *Why I Am Catholic (and You Should Be Too)*

"The ongoing debate within the Church about the Second Vatican Council serves as a microcosm of our age: well-meaning, passionate people have divided themselves into camps, so sure of their own positions that they are unable to hear the truth spoken by the other. Fr. Blake Britton offers a balanced, grounded response that our Church desperately needs. Correctly identifying Vatican II as a 'kerygmatic' council, he invites the reader to let go of half-truths and learn from the documents themselves in order to behold the splendor of the Church."

Fr. Casey Cole, O.F.M.
Creator of Breaking in the Habit Media

"This timely little book could not come at a more opportune moment. Polarization over the Second Vatican Council has reached a new degree of intensity, at least in the public eye. I continue to have the faith that, as Fr. Blake Britton suggests, the documents of Vatican II—spirit, content, and all—can still today provide the inspiration for meaningful reform in the Church and for the evangelization of the modern world."

From the foreword by **John C. Cavadini**
McGrath-Cavadini director of the McGrath Institute for Church Life
University of Notre Dame

RECLAIMING

WHAT IT (REALLY) SAID, WHAT IT MEANS,

VATICAN II

AND HOW IT CALLS US TO RENEW THE CHURCH

FR. BLAKE BRITTON
FOREWORD BY JOHN C. CAVADINI

Ave Maria Press AVE Notre Dame, Indiana

WORD on FIRE

© 2021 by Blake Britton

All rights reserved. No part of this book may be used or reproduced in any manner whatsoever, except in the case of reprints in the context of reviews, without written permission from Ave Maria Press®, Inc., P.O. Box 428, Notre Dame, IN 46556, 1-800-282-1865.

Founded in 1865, Ave Maria Press is a ministry of the United States Province of Holy Cross.

www.avemariapress.com

Paperback: ISBN-13 978-1-64680-029-2

E-book: ISBN-13 978-1-64680-030-8

Cover image © David Lees / The LIFE Images Collection / Getty Images.

Cover and text design by Christopher D. Tobin.

Printed and bound in the United States of America.

Library of Congress Cataloging-in-Publication Data
Names: Britton, Blake, author.
Title: Reclaiming Vatican II : what it (really) said, what it means, and
   how it calls us to renew the church / Blake Britton.
Description: Notre Dame, Indiana : Ave Maria Press, [2021] | Includes
   bibliographical references. | Summary: "Throughout this book, the author
   clears up misconceptions about the Second Vatican Council and reveals
   how-when properly understood and applied-it fosters a richer experience
   of being the Church"-- Provided by publisher.
Identifiers: LCCN 2021022247 | ISBN 9781646800292 (paperback) | ISBN
   9781646800308 (ebook)
Subjects: LCSH: Vatican Council (2nd : 1962-1965 : Basilica di San Pietro
   in Vaticano) | Catholic Church--Doctrines. | Church renewal--Catholic
   Church. | BISAC: RELIGION / Christianity / Catholic | RELIGION /
   Christian Theology / History
Classification: LCC BX830 1962 .B686 2021 | DDC 262/.52--dc23
LC record available at https://lccn.loc.gov/2021022247

Dedicated to Pope Emeritus Benedict XVI
and all the Fathers of the Second Vatican Council.
May the work the Holy Spirit began in you be brought to
completion in the hearts of God's People.

CONTENTS

FOREWORD

This timely little book could not come at a more opportune moment. Polarization over the Second Vatican Council has reached a new degree of intensity, at least in the public eye. Some prominent prelates of the Church are calling for the rejection of the council altogether, on the grounds that at many points it is at variance with inherited Church teaching, both in letter and in spirit. On the other hand, equally prominent "liberal" interpreters of the council are promoting a wholesale rejection of the letter of the documents in favor of revisionary teaching that represents the true "spirit" of the council, or, what the Council *would have taught* if it were not bound by the need to compromise with prominent reactionaries who worked hard to completely block any changes that they perceived to be too "modernist."

These latter "liberals" are styled as "paraconciliar" by Fr. Britton, meaning that the council they "received" and handed on was not Vatican II itself but a "paracouncil" assembled from the views of dissenting theologians, uninformed and biased media, and from the very cultural tendencies, such as pervasive secularization, which Vatican II was called to address. The paracouncil, in effect, replaced the teaching of the council with its own ideologies. It therefore occluded much of the actual, concrete teaching of the council on matters such as the use of Latin in the Mass, the nature and character of priestly ministry, and its relationship to the royal priesthood of the baptized, the place of Mary in the life of the Church, the way in which the scriptures should be interpreted, and more. So thoroughly did the ideas of the paracouncil eclipse the ideas of the actual council, that most Catholics came to believe these were the ideas of the actual council. Some, then, in reaction to the paraconciliar ideas that masqueraded as the council itself, have promoted, in Fr. Britton's language, a "traditionalist" back-lash against the council—or, at least, against what they *think* is the council and its teaching.

In fact, as Fr. Britton so accurately points out, neither camp seems to know the documents themselves very well. The documents seem largely to have been left behind in the heat and fury of competing views. It is not remembered that *Sacrosanctum Concilium*, for example, did not call for the wholesale rejection of Latin in the liturgy, but expected that in some ways it would remain normative. Similarly, the calls for inculturation of the liturgy were not intended to displace Gregorian chant or other expressions of the universal Church's one voice. The council did not even mandate celebration of the Mass facing the people. Nor did *Lumen Gentium* use the phrase "people of God" as a new name for the laity, nor did it envision a flattening out of the sacramental, ministerial priest-hood through a quasi-Protestant "leveling" effect relative to the priesthood of all the baptized. Nor did *Lumen Gentium* displace Marian devotion by reducing it to an afterthought of ecclesiology or a kind of optional practice to be henceforth relegated solely under the category of "popular devotion," meaning it was okay for the uneducated or those from non-Anglo cultures, but otherwise outgrown by the more "enlightened."

My own views on these matters are available elsewhere, so I will not take them up here.[1] Instead, I'd like to provide in this foreword a kind of repayment of a debt. A debt of love and gratitude for the council itself, congruent, as I see it, with the sentiments advanced by Fr. Britton in his call for a recovery and a deeper appreciation of the actual vision of the council.

Fr. Britton points out that the time will soon come when no one is left who will remember being at the council, no one whose life will have encompassed both an experience of the council and an experience of its aftermath. I was too young to be present at the council, but I do remember its earliest implementation, as I was fourteen years old when the council concluded. I was too young to care about, or even know about, Church politics, but not too young to have had a vivid impression of the liturgical reforms as they were phased in. I was absolutely thrilled. My grandmother was not. Repeatedly, she voiced her distaste, regret, and apprehension at the systematic, though gradual, obsolescence of Latin in favor of English, as well as at the reforms in gesture, manner of celebrating, and so on.

I could not understand her concerns. I do remember realizing, with some dim sense of alarm, that this was a point of no return, and I remember regretting that there would no longer be a universal liturgical language in the Church. But these feelings were overshadowed by the enthusiasm I felt for finally being able to understand the Mass and to experience it as a living act in which I could participate directly. The Mass had not seemed to be "mine" in any significant way, but rather something that was done, principally, by the specialists in the sanctuary, the priest and servers. We were not *just* observers, but the sense that we were not just observers was to a large extent dependent on the parts of the Mass that *were* in English and facing the people, namely, the Gospel reading, the homily, and the announcements. The Last Gospel was also in English, and, though it was not read facing the people, I did feel I participated in that weighty moment of utter solemnity and felt a special love for it because I could understand it in all of its poetical gravity.

Couldn't we have followed along in the Missal, in English translation, you might ask? Well, yes—that is, if you could even hear the priest. It was nice that now, due to the reforms, we would be able to *hear* the Mass celebrated. To a varying extent, the prayers of the priest were then often said in a low voice that was inaudible, especially since the words were spoken by someone turned away from the assembly. Also, to read a translation is at the same time to be aware that one is, by that very fact, in some significant sense, "outside" the celebration, which would be otherwise inaccessible.

So many other "markers" seemed to reinforce that feeling of being "outside." Even the sense of reverence and awe associated with the Eucharist could itself be another marker that the Eucharist belonged, essentially, to the priests, whose hands had been specially anointed, as the nuns preparing us for First Communion had told us, while ours had not been. One would no sooner think of picking up a dropped host, should something so unthinkable ever occur, than of painting graffiti on the church walls. Along with the (appropriate) feeling of being unworthy of the Eucharist, there was the additional feeling of somehow being intrinsically impure, ritually impure, which is different entirely. My grandmother, I remember, went to communion only once a year, to do her Easter Duty, at the last possible moment, and she brushed not only her teeth that morning, but her tongue.

The change to English, and to the posture of facing the people, made me feel as though I were accepted and included in this very important and sacred act. I felt as though I belonged, and that it was important that I played my part, and that the liturgy would in some way be lessened (though just as efficacious sacramentally) if I did not. I am a cradle Catholic of the most "standard" variety. I have no dramatic stories of conversion or mystical experiences to report, but simply the dull gratitude for being a member of a Church I am sure I would have not had the courage to join if God had not, in his love, seen fit to bring me into this life in an extended family of practicing believers. I'm a member of the lay faithful, ordinary in every way.

Yet, I remember one moment of special intensity. For some reason one Sunday I had taken home a monthly "missalette" and during the week began to read the text of the Mass in English from start to finish. I was startled by the beauty of the prayers, by their warmth, their intimacy, and their giving voice to things that seemed to matter to all people. I remember for some reason dwelling especially on the Agnus Dei and on the collects. I must have spent a half hour in rapt attention, my heart filling with the warmth of the liturgical words. I felt a true joy and elation at the beautiful words that were prescribed for *me* to say or to listen to attentively. That feeling has never left me. It was the closest thing to an interior "conversion" that I can recall. And even when I am in a foreign country and the liturgy is in a language I do not know, I still "understand" it because I can say it to myself in English, these beautiful things, these same sentiments full of nobility, dignity, and gratitude.

Later on, as a sophomore at a very secular liberal arts college, I remember, almost in desperation for something less cynical and more idealistic than anything on offer in many of the texts read in my classes, picking up a copy of the documents of Vatican II. I opened them at random and lit upon *Gaudium et Spes*. Though it was a seeming waste of time, because I got no course credit for it and certainly no recognition, I could not put the text down. I just kept reading and could not get enough. The questions raised were *my* questions! And the *Church* was interested in them! My soul was lit on fire with the Church's confidence that she had the answers to these questions and could offer a repository of wisdom that rose above the relativism of the so-called learned discourse that denied human dignity or could express it only in one-dimensional, Marxist terms. Going on to *Lumen Gentium*, my heart was indelibly marked, I felt, by the sublimity of the teaching of the "universal call to holiness." I wanted to live up to that. I felt fixed in that ideal. Reading chapter 5 of *Lumen Gentium* ignited a kind of zeal in me and even today I still feel it, and I reread that chapter with ever-new gratitude, every time I have occasion to teach this text.

Reading these documents was motivation enough for me to start going to daily Mass, to visit the Blessed Sacrament in between times, and also to picket the local A&P on Saturday mornings in solidarity with the United Farmworkers Union. I also came to decide that, although I did not feel a vocation to the priesthood, I could contribute to evangelization through the "return to the sources" and the recovery of their teaching in a way attuned to modern questions, as a theologian. My heart was on fire to do so, and, to tell the truth, it still is. That is the debt of gratitude and love that I owe to Vatican II: my whole life as an adult Catholic.

Turning back to the categories of reception that Fr. Britton lays out: With regard to the "traditionalists," I think many of them—especially the younger of them, many of whom belong to the professional, educated social sectors—underestimate how much they owe to the very council they sometimes seem to want to disown. The sense that the Tridentine Latin liturgy is more aesthetic and more reverent is partly a function of the reforms of Vatican II that moved away from a culture that routinely permitted twenty-minute Masses hastily said *sotto voce* and without a homily. Further, these beautiful younger people experience the Tridentine Mass with Vatican II sensibilities that they simply take for granted, namely, that they are included as an important constituent of the celebration of the Mass, and are not just, in effect, second-class participants observing from the perspective of the vaguely ritually-impure spectator.

On the other hand, as for the paracouncil, the more I was drawn into the documents of Vatican II, especially as I began to use them to teach, the more I was struck by the "silence" that seemed imposed on the documents, selectively, in public discourse and theological literature. For example, the *Catechism of the Catholic Church* was critiqued upon its publication for not having a sufficiently critically informed sense of scripture in accordance with *Dei Verbum*, while the *Catechism*'s extensive use of the "analogy of faith" and the sense of scripture as a whole precisely as called for by *Dei Verbum* was left without comment, in silence. In fact, the *Catechism* uses scripture in exactly the same way as the documents of Vatican II themselves. Particularly jarring was the way in which, as Fr. Britton notes, the council called for the continuing relevance of Latin as a liturgical language, when in fact it came to be a mark of one's liturgical backwardness to even suggest that Latin should have some kind of continued presence in the public prayer of the Church. The Church in the United States seems to lack imagination in comparison with many of the African churches that manage to combine Latin and the vernacular in ways that display a connection to the most ancient traditions—in contrast to the Pentecostal churches that compete for the allegiance of Catholics—while setting them in the context of an authentic African sensibility.

Overall, however, I have had the faith, and continue to have the faith that, as Fr. Britton suggests, the documents of Vatican II—spirit, content, and all—can still today provide the inspiration for meaningful reform in the Church and for the evangelization of the "modern world." This work will not be accomplished in the glare of publicity, as though media attention were what made it important, but rather without fanfare, in the implementation, little by little, of the vision of the council in the ordinary life of the parish. This will mean the patient cultivation of a liturgical sensibility of awe, and yes, unworthiness, at the lavishly loving sacrifice of the Lord, accomplished on the Cross and still poured out for us even today in the Eucharist. This is not primarily the awe of an aesthetic, but the awe at a mystery of love of which indeed we are not worthy and therefore for which we learn to be more and more grateful. Let this awe spill over into the related awe at the dignity of the human person and of the beauty of the world that "God so loved" that sacrifice of Christ's Precious Blood was not unthinkable. The works of love and mercy in response—for example, the work of parenting and of caring for the poor and for those in need of comfort—are also not glamorous. They are often hidden and seemingly inefficient. But all of this provides the ingredients of a renewal of culture based in faith, truth, and beauty, that can truly be, over time, a persuasive response to the "joys and hopes, the griefs and anxieties" of our own world, at the same time so precious and so troubled.

John C. Cavadini

ACKNOWLEDGMENTS

At the very foundations of the Christian life is a single word, *Eucharist*, which means "thanksgiving." Gratitude constitutes the basis of our faith, the recognition that all things are given by the Father, through the Son, in the unity of the Holy Spirit: "What do you have that you did not receive?" (1 Cor 4:7). For my part, I have received much from the Father's goodness and I will spend the rest of my priesthood attempting to respond to his gracious favor. Thus, before all else, I thank God for this book and the many people and experiences which he allowed to influence its inception. To his glory, I consecrate this work and all the deeds of my life, and I pray that everything I do is for the sake of Jesus Christ and the Church.

I also thank and honor our Blessed Mother. Her constant intercession and maternal love is the guiding of star of my discipleship. I daily turn to her as an example of obedience and humility before the will of God. May she always remain with me in the Christian journey.

The influence of my family cannot be overstated. My mother's untiring service to the Church, keen theological mind, and unbreakable faith in Christ was my first encounter with Catholicism. If it were not for her, I would never know the name of Jesus; there is no greater gift anyone has given me. I will forever love her as the first Christian I ever met and an amazing mother.

To my father, I owe my sense of duty and courage as a man. From boyhood, he instilled within my soul a profound attitude of strength, honor, and responsibility that must never compromise the truth nor quell before any task. I only pray I can love the Church with the same masculine virtue with which he loves our family.

To my siblings, Alexander, Jacob, and Victoria, I will never be able to express how each of you have formed my priestly heart. I would not be the man I am today without you. Being your big brother remains one of the greatest joys of my life.

In addition to my family, there are countless people whose knowledge, expertise, and support have gone into the composition of this book. First among these is my local ordinary, Bishop John Noonan, and the people of the Diocese of Orlando. Thanks to Msgr. David Page, whose enthusiasm for Vatican II inspired me to begin this project. Likewise, I want to acknowledge Bishop Robert Barron and my dear friends at Word on Fire. Thank you to Brandon and Kathleen Vogt, Jason and Rachel Bulman, my Iesu Caritas brothers, Dr. John Cavadini, Dr. Troy Stefano, Dr. Mary Soho, Mr. Tony Arza, Fr. Ivan Olmo, Fr. Juan Osorno, and the many others without whose friendship I could not have hoped to write this work.

Finally, I want to thank Ave Maria Press for their leadership and guidance in this endeavor. Most especially, I recognize Mr. Daniel Marrs, whose patience, enthusiasm, and professionalism has left an impression on me that will not soon be forgotten.

God bless you all!

INTRODUCTION

Few topics in the Church today rattle and divide as much as the Second Vatican Council. Fifty years after its conclusion, we are still debating Vatican II's intention and meaning. This is not entirely unprecedented. Lengthy periods of deliberation typically follow any Church council. As one bishop told me, "It takes several decades even to scratch the surface of a council, let alone adequately understand and apply its teachings." That being said, most Catholics can agree that the implementation of Vatican II has been less than ideal.

I began to recognize this as a young seminarian. While I was serving at a parish in Florida, the retired pastor, Msgr. David Page, invited me out for lunch. In the course of our conversation, Msgr. Page noted that his first appointment as a newly ordained priest was a secretarial position to Archbishop Joseph Patrick Hurley, then bishop of St. Augustine, Florida. Msgr. Page accompanied the bishop during his various episcopal ventures, including his participation in the Second Vatican Council. Over several hours, Msgr. Page regaled me with stories about the inner workings of Vatican II. I was utterly fascinated—and inspired to begin researching the council for myself. That research turned into a decade-long study. During that time, I read every document promulgated by Vatican II as well as numerous schemas, commentaries, journals, and letters written by people present at the sessions.

As my study progressed, I started to notice something both perplexing and unsettling, namely, a wide discrepancy between what was taught by the council fathers and what is commonly promoted at the parochial level. What I read in the documents was beautiful, theological, and orthodox. But much of what I witnessed being done in "the spirit of Vatican II" was quite the contrary.

This realization reoriented my research. I needed to understand not only what had happened at the council but why there has been such a persistent disconnect between its teachings and the general interpretations of those teachings. I finally found my answer in an unexpected source.

While reading Henri de Lubac's outstanding little book, *A Brief Catechesis on Nature and Grace*, I stumbled across the appendices. There in Appendix C, I spotted an essay entitled "The Council and the Paracouncil." From the moment I read the first paragraph, I knew I had discovered something vital for unraveling what happened after Vatican II:

> Just as the Second Vatican Council received from a number of theologians instructions about various points of the task it should assume, under the pain of "disappointing the world," so too the "post-conciliar" Church was immediately and from all sides assailed with summons to get in step, *not with what the Council had actually said*, but with what it *should* have said. . . . This is the phenomenon which we should like to designate as the "paracouncil." . . . Among many people, whether partisans or opponents or simply docile followers (all of whom were equally fooled), this paracouncil, which often deserved the name "anti-Council," has been mistaken for the true Council; and whatever in the latter's work did not correspond with the former's program has more than once been neglected or misrepresented.[1]

De Lubac goes on to explain the far-reaching effects of this paracouncil: "What the paracouncil and its main activists wanted and demanded was a *mutation* [of the council]: a difference not of degree, but of nature."[2]

After reading this paragraph, everything clicked for me. De Lubac's distinction between the council and the paracouncil provided not only a lucid paradigm by which to understand the inconsistency between the council's teaching and post-conciliar practice, but also a lens through which to view the factions that have developed within the Church since the council.

On the one hand, we have so-called liberal Catholics who, under the auspices of the paracouncil, believe Vatican II opened the doors to a more modern theology. They encourage dismantling the "tired traditions" and "close-minded beliefs" of the pre–Vatican II Church. As a result, numerous aspects of the faith have been muddled and disenfranchised. Liturgy is seen as a self-gratifying enterprise where the satisfaction of our egos dictates the music, preaching, church architecture, and celebration of the Eucharist. Social justice is reduced to simple activism. The Catholic identity of our schools and universities is repressed in favor of a more "progressive" and "inclusive" environment unconstrained by religious doctrine. Thus, in a well-meaning but misguided attempt to relate positively to contemporary society, the genius of Catholicity is supplanted by nonspiritual ideals. This "reverse catechesis" has been a disaster. As a result, millions of Catholics are leaving the Church as she seemingly fades into irrelevance, just one sentimental institution among many in our culture.

On the other hand, many "conservative" or "traditional" Catholics are in all-out rebellion against Vatican II or, more appropriately, what is falsely peddled as Vatican II. Witnessing the deterioration of solemnity, piety, and catechesis in parishes across the world, they seek to circle the wagons by returning to the tried-and-true infrastructures of traditional Catholicism. In so doing, they hope to revive the Church's past glory so that she can reassert her unique presence in the world. This is verified by the growing number of young men and women who are opting for the traditional Latin liturgy, seeing it in opposition to the liturgy of Vatican II. Many of the people attracted to this conservative mindset are driven by a deep sense of woundedness and frustration with their local parish experience. Far from being contrarian or close-minded Catholics (although some of them are), the majority simply desire orthodoxy, clarity, reverence, and beauty. In an age when truth is relative, tradition is suspect, and beauty is marred, these men and women are seeking a bedrock of holiness for themselves and their children. Seemingly, the only place to find such stability is "traditional" Catholicism, which often shuns the Second Vatican Council and the follies that presumably flowed from it.

But here's what de Lubac helped me see: In the end, neither of these groups is responding to the Second Vatican Council itself. They are both reacting to the *paracouncil,* either accepting or rejecting this poor caricature of what the council actually taught and envisioned. For example, "liberals" are often told that Vatican II was a new beginning in the life of the Church, calling for a rejection of old-style Catholicism so as to create a more relatable form of the faith. "Conservatives" are often told Vatican II suppressed Latin and *ad orientem,* disavowed orthodox theology, or paved the way for the perversion of our religion. None of these claims are correct.

The tension between these two camps has disproportionately influenced the last fifty years of theological discussion and liturgical praxis since the council. As a result, the council has become a flashpoint of controversy for many people while the vast majority of Catholics remain indifferent about Vatican II and are left on the sidelines.

But what if there is another way to understand Vatican II? That question brings us to the purpose of this book. I assert that there *is* another way—and that way lies within a reclamation of the genuine intentions of the Second Vatican Council's teachings. There must be a return to the authentic texts of Vatican II "without reservations that amputate them and without arbitrariness that distorts them."[3] The following pages attempt to carry out that task.

Transcending the political categories of left and right, we will explore the essential nature of Vatican II, with the goal of promoting a constructive and contemplative conversation. This necessitates dispelling several myths about the council that are commonly pushed by either liberal or conservative outlets. At the same time, we will need to discuss with candor what took place in the years immediately following the council that caused these myths to emerge.

To readers who identify as liberal and progressive: You can take great joy in knowing that Vatican II invites and revitalizes the spirit of innovation—but it does so in a way that's more deeply continuous with tradition than you might have realized.

To conservative and traditionalist readers: Vatican II does not seek to repress or dismiss any of the heritage that you know and love. In truth, it not only supports our great tradition, but seeks a reengagement with scripture and the Church Fathers, providing an even stronger foothold by which to build on the faith and wisdom of our forebears.

Finally, to the millions of Catholics today who don't fit neatly into polarized political categories: This book is for you in a special way. I meet so many of you in my daily ministry as a priest. I am inspired to find among you a generation of Christians who understand that being Catholic transcends the categories of liberal and conservative. In the words of Bishop Robert Barron, you are a generation who is "both progressive and conservative, both stubbornly alive and stubbornly traditional."[4] Your hearts long for a balanced, orthodox, and vibrant Catholicism that may sometimes seem like an unreachable ideal. But I assure you it is not! The Holy Spirit desires the same thing and has provided the recipe for it through the Second Vatican Council.

The following words from Joseph Ratzinger (the future Pope Benedict XVI) summarize the mission set before us with piercing clarity:

> I believe . . . the true time of Vatican II has not yet come,
> that its authentic reception has not yet begun: its doc-
> uments were quickly buried under a pile of superficial
> or frankly inexact publications. The reading of the *letter*
> of the documents will enable us to discover their true
> *spirit*. If thus rediscovered in their truth, those great
> texts will make it possible for us to understand just what
> happened and to react with a new vigor. . . . The Catholic
> who clearly and, consequently, painfully perceives the
> damage that has been wrought in his Church by the
> misinterpretation of Vatican II must find the possibility
> of revival in Vatican II itself.[5]

Reclaiming Vatican II is not simply a *possible* avenue of reforming and refocusing the Church; it is *the* avenue, provided by the
Holy Spirit himself through the Mystical Body of Christ. Our duty
is to trust in the Lord's inspiration, giving ourselves to what has
been given to us so that *his* will may be done.

Soon enough, there will be no one alive who actually attended
the Second Vatican Council. It will fall on the shoulders of younger
generations, especially millennials like myself, to implement the
vision inspired by the Holy Spirit at Vatican II.

The fruition of a council is a responsibility that has been
entrusted to only a few select generations. We are one such generation. After more than fifty years of trial and error, we have
learned many lessons and grown in understanding. Now is the
time to reclaim Vatican II, allowing the full fruits of its graces to
blossom in the hearts of God's people. The task is daunting, to be
sure, but simultaneously invigorating. In every age, Catholics must
choose how to actualize their call to sainthood. Will you join me
in choosing to be a saint of Vatican II, a saint who obediently seeks
to build a legacy for those who come after us so that they might
enjoy the graces of God's will? My prayer is that this generation
will take up the mantle of evangelization and reclaim Vatican II.
Only then can the full sum of its graces be shared with the world.

ABBREVIATIONS

CCC .... *Catechism of the Catholic Church.* Libreria Editrice Vaticana, 1992. Vatican Archive, https://www.vatican.va/archive/ENG0015/_INDEX.HTM.

DV .... Vatican Council II, *Dei Verbum* (Word of God). Edited by Austin Flannery. New York: Costello Publishing Co., 2004.

GS .... Vatican Council II, *Gaudium et Spes* (Joy and Hope). Edited by Austin Flannery. New York: Costello Publishing Co., 2004.

LG .... Vatican Council II, *Lumen Gentium* (Light of the Nations). Edited by Austin Flannery. New York: Costello Publishing Co., 2004.

SSC .... Vatican Council II, *Sacrosanctum Concilium* (On the Sacred Liturgy). Edited by Austin Flannery. New York: Costello Publishing Co., 2004.

UR .... Vatican Council II, *Unitatis Redintegratio* (Restoration of Unity). Edited by Austin Flannery. New York: Costello Publishing Co., 2004.

1

THE PARACOUNCIL: WHAT HAPPENED?

At the heart of this book is a simple message: The Church today must reclaim the legacy of the Second Vatican Council. Vatican II is *the* avenue for reforming and refocusing the Church. But before we can do that, we need to look a little more closely at why the council needs to be reclaimed in the first place.

Vatican II is a point of contention for many within the Church. Tensions permeate social media and other places of discourse in the Catholic world, with traditional and liberal Catholics disagreeing about Vatican II's supposed implications for liturgy, catechesis, the Church's relationship with the world, and more.

But both sides are laboring under some serious misunderstandings. As outlined in the introduction, both liberal and traditional camps are responding to what Henri de Lubac calls "the paracouncil"—a poor caricature of what the council really taught and envisioned. Thus, before we can reintroduce ourselves to Vatican II's true spirit and begin to reclaim its legacy for the Church, we need to get a better handle on what led to such a massive misimplementation and misrepresentation of the council's vision.

The story behind the rise of the paracouncil is complex. Beginning with specific individuals who used Vatican II as an opportunity to endorse personal theologies, it quickly morphed into an en masse counternarrative. I have found it useful to identify three aspects of the rise of the paracouncil: 1) the council of the theologians, 2) the council of the media, and 3) the council of the age.

The Council of the Theologians

One of the biggest factors in the rise of the paracouncil was theologians setting themselves up as deputized interpreters of Vatican II—and of Church teaching as a whole. Then-cardinal Joseph Ratzinger offers a clear summary of this phenomenon: "After the Council . . . theologians increasingly felt themselves to be the true teachers of the Church and even of the bishops. Moreover, since the Council they had been discovered by mass media and had captured their interest."[1] For some theologians, the council documents failed to embody the radical change they hoped Vatican II would achieve. In their opinion, these documents represented half-baked compromises that sought to appease certain factions among the council fathers.

The "Spirit" of Vatican II

Their solution to this perceived shortcoming of the council's documents? Instead of adhering to the documents of the council, some theologians opted to follow what they called "the spirit of Vatican II." You can probably see where this is headed. In setting aside the texts and focusing instead on the council's "spirit," "a vast margin was left open for the question on how this spirit should subsequently be defined and room was consequently made for every whim."[2] In lieu of promoting the documents as written and in cooperation with the magisterium, certain theologians presented the teaching of the council through the lens of their own theological agenda, foisting themselves on public opinion as authentic interpreters of the council.[3]

This clearly contradicts the proper vocation of a theologian. Theologians are not freelance agents or self-appointed judges of the magisterium. Before all else they are humble servants "officially charged with the task of presenting and illustrating the doctrine of the faith *in its integrity and with full accuracy*."[4] However, that ideal was not upheld by various theologians in the years following Vatican II.

One example of this phenomenon: In 1967 (two years after the closing sessions of Vatican II), the Belgian theologian Edward Schillebeeckx published a book commenting on the council's document *Lumen Gentium*. In it, he celebrates the Second Vatican Council's definition of the Church as the "sacrament of the world," calling this understanding of the Church "one of the most charismatic to come out of Vatican II."[5]

The problem? The Second Vatican Council did not use the phrase "sacrament of the world" a single time in any of its documents! In fact, this term was deliberately excluded by the council, which instead referred to the Church as the "sacrament of salvation" (*LG* 48). I'll elaborate on exactly what was at stake in that distinction between "sacrament of the world" and "sacrament of salvation" later. But for now, we use the example to demonstrate one startling point: The council taught one thing, and a highly influential theologian openly taught another—while claiming faithfulness to the actual intention of Vatican II. On the heels of the council, Schillebeeckx willfully conflated the message of Vatican II with his own personal opinion.

Sadly, this was not an isolated case. Within the first ten years after the council, popular, influential figures in the Church performed the same parlor trick over and over again in publications and lectures, disseminating their personal theological ideas as faithful expressions of the Second Vatican Council. What's more, numerous universities and seminaries were quickly subverted by these misrepresentations. Students and seminarians, rather than immersing themselves in the council texts and seeking to understand them at face value, were *told* what to believe about Vatican II, thus being formed in the so-called spirit of the council.

The fallout was significant—and its effects continue to this day. Pope emeritus Benedict XVI alluded to this in his recent letter, "The Church and the Scandal of Sexual Abuse." While reflecting on the negative influences of seminary formation in the immediate post-conciliar years, he writes:

> The long-prepared and ongoing process of dissolution of the Christian concept of morality was, as I have tried to show, marked by an unprecedented radicalism in the 1960s. . . . Indeed, in many parts of the Church, conciliar attitudes were understood to mean having a critical or negative attitude towards the hitherto existing tradition, which was now to be replaced by a new, radically open relationship with the world. . . . There were . . . individual bishops who rejected the Catholic tradition as a whole and sought to bring about a kind of new, modern "Catholicity" in their dioceses.[6]

This "conciliar attitude" spoken of by the pope emeritus is often referred to as the "spirit of Vatican II." In reality, however, many of the things done in the so-called spirit of Vatican II are quite contrary to the actual teachings of the council. I'll always remember what one bishop told me during a retreat: "If a person says their theology or program is done in the 'spirit Vatican II,' it most likely isn't."

The council as interpreted by these theologians became a counternarrative to the official magisterium of the Church. Unsurprisingly, a rift of resentment formed between the "freethinking" academics in universities, seminaries, parishes, and schools and the "close-minded authoritarian" hierarchy of the Church. We can still feel the effects of this division in our parishes and institutions today.

An Example: Latin Language and Vatican II

It is difficult to overstate just how influentially and efficiently the so-called spirit of Vatican II has circulated throughout Catholic culture in the past five decades, causing considerable confusion along the way. Take, for example, the common misconception that Vatican II suppressed the use of Latin in the Mass. In fact, nothing could be further from the truth, as we'll see in chapter 3! But for both those who love and appreciate liturgical Latin and those who have joyfully welcomed celebrating Mass in their own language, misunderstandings about Vatican II's teachings on the matter continue to run rampant.

Recently, I had an interaction with a graduate from one of our Catholic universities in the United States. She has a master's degree in theology. In the course of our conversation, it became clear that she believed Vatican II had suppressed the use of Latin in the sacred liturgy—and that anyone who still valued liturgical Latin was out of step with Vatican II. When I asked her which documents of the council banned or discouraged Latin, she reluctantly admitted that in all her years of study she'd never read any of the actual council documents. A professor had assured her that Latin was against the "spirit" of the council and an obstacle to the Church "moving forward."

On the other side of the aisle, I spoke with a traditionalist seminarian several years ago at the March for Life in Washington, DC. We walked and conversed with each other for nearly an hour. What I found most interesting was that he also claimed Vatican II had suppressed the use of Latin in the Mass. I asked him the same question about where he read this in the council documents and received the same response. He had not read any of them.

Even a cursory reading of the council documents would go a long way toward answering many of the critiques hurled against Vatican II. Throughout years of conversations and debates, I've discovered time and time again that most people who say they agree or disagree with the teachings, theology, and practices of Vatican II are actually agreeing or disagreeing with the interpretations of specific theologians—not the publications of the council itself.

The Council of the Media

We are not strangers to the concept of "fake news." Mass media outlets are prone to morph reports about current events to fit a specific narrative their network wants to push. Believe it or not, this took place just as much in 1963 as it does in our own time. Such was the case with the Second Vatican Council. In a decade already brimming with excitement about societal revolution, the council proved enticing. Matthew L. Lamb and Matthew Levering provide an enlightening summary of the media's role in interpreting the council:

> Never before was an ecumenical council of the Roman Catholic Church so extensively covered and reported by the modern news media as Vatican II (1962–1965). The impact of this coverage was pervasive and profound in its portrayal of the council in the ideological categories of "liberal and conservative." The council was dramatically reported as a liberal or progressive accommodation to modernity that aimed to overcome Catholicism's traditional, conservative resistance to modernity. . . . Journalists of the print and electronic media flocked to Rome. Few had any expertise in Catholic theology and so were dependent upon popularized accounts of the council's deliberations and debates offered by *periti* [conciliar theological consultants] and theologians with journalistic skills.[7]

Lamb and Levering highlight two important points. The first we discussed above, namely, the media becoming a mouthpiece for theologians promoting their personal interpretations of the council. The second was just as damaging: the media's parceling of the Church into liberal and conservative factions.

The Liberal-versus-Conservative Narrative

It is wholly inadequate to interpret events in the life of the Church through a secular society's political categories. The Church intersects constantly with our daily social and political realities—but we must remember that it is a divine institution that must be understood in a spiritual way. To restrictively cipher Church actions as nothing more than a skirmish between liberal and conservative groups will always prove insufficient and lopsided. Yet, that is exactly what the media did when reporting on Vatican II.

Both during and after the council, journalists constructed a dramatized narrative detailing supposed clashes between liberal and conservative blocs behind the walls of St. Peter's. Media outlets sought to portray Vatican II as a battle between progressive freethinkers and close-minded traditionalists. News reports that catered to this simplistic liberal-versus-conservative story line tantalized people's imaginations. For months, headlines poured out from the council giving a play-by-play analysis of the bishops' proceedings. Disagreements were exaggerated, partial information was leaked prematurely, and pseudo-truths were reported.

This is not to say the council was free of conflict and completely cordial. The memoirs of *periti* such as Louis Bouyer and Henri de Lubac are enough to dispel that notion. But to depict the council as a fight between two warring ideologies is certainly deficient. The truth of the matter is much more nuanced.

Unfortunately, the media's tendency to see conflicts through a liberal-versus-conservative lens is still hurting the Church in our own time. Media reports on synods, papal meetings, and bishops' conferences are covered more like American politics than spiritual gatherings. As a result, certain topics become triggers that immediately cast people into a frenzy, thus compromising our ability to dialogue and think critically about important subjects. This is because the press uses "categories from the world, and they don't fully appreciate that [the Church is] dealing with a different way of being, a different way of thinking."[8] The Church's discourse must transcend the limiting dichotomies of conservative and liberal. Truth must be the Church's only concern, not appealing to a Gallup poll or appeasing a political faction.

Even Catholic media sometimes succumb to the liberal-versus-conservative mindset. Certain religious news agencies thrive on manufactured drama between the liberal and conservative camps. Likewise, many laypersons and clergy on social media are constantly at odds with one another, at times even falling into slander and defamation. I believe this to be a pressing spiritual danger for our generation, especially for those within the Church who are seeking legitimate reform.

One of the consequences of this polarized discourse is the constant undercutting of sincere attempts to live and minister in accord with Vatican II. For example, if a priest wants to start celebrating the ordinary form of the Mass in Latin twice a year so as to be in accord with the council's directive to accustom the faithful to the Latin language, he is immediately dubbed a conservative traditionalist even though he celebrates Mass in the vernacular the other 363 days of the year. Yet, if that same priest says something positive about Pope Francis in a Sunday homily, he is dubbed a liberal progressive who hates tradition. In reality, he is just a *Catholic* priest, a man seeking beauty, goodness, and truth wherever it is to be found, and obedient to whatever forms the Church offers it to the world.

If we are to reclaim Vatican II and continue striving toward authentic renewal, we must broaden our horizons and break out of the restrictive categories of liberal and conservative. A layperson who likes the Mass in Latin is not a conservative Catholic any more than a layperson who likes "On Eagle's Wings" is a liberal Catholic. They are both simply Catholics seeking Christ.

That being said, I am not advocating for some type of relativism. There are proper and improper ways to practice Catholicism. But in order to discern appropriate forms of orthodoxy ("right belief") and orthopraxis ("right practice"), we must be free of triggers as well as uncharitable presuppositions about others' opinions and motives.

In the end, this can only be accomplished through love. For "love unites us to God . . . has no limits to its endurance, bears everything patiently. Love is neither servile nor arrogant. It does not provoke schisms or form cliques, but always acts in harmony with others."[9] These words from Pope St. Clement are timeless, applying even to our current situation. We must presume the goodness of the other even if that goodness is misguided or confused. Doing so affords us the patience necessary for true dialogue.

Go to the Sources

There is another reason for the media's powerful influence that speaks to a deeper problem with modern education as a whole, namely, our willingness to rely on secondhand reports and summaries of important topics.

In addition to my ministry as a parish priest, I am a teacher. One of the first things I teach my students is to rely on primary sources over secondary sources. If you are studying George Washington, don't just read a textbook paragraph or a Wikipedia article about him. Instead, read one of his letters or his inaugural speeches. If you are studying Dante Alighieri, read the *Divine Comedy*. If you are studying Antonio Vivaldi, listen to one of his concertos. Enter into an intellectual relationship with the person's work and make a preliminary judgment based on that encounter. Only after you take this fundamental step can you begin a healthy engagement with secondary resources and listen to various opinions.

Most people get this backward. We start with the secondary sources before turning to the primary—or worse yet, never bother with the primary at all—with the result that ignorance proliferates. This most certainly happened (and continues to happen) with the Second Vatican Council via mass media and social media. When I listen to analyses of the council from different media outlets or

YouTube videos, I cannot help but call to mind the exasperation of Shakespeare's Holofernes in *Love's Labour's Lost*: "O thou monster, Ignorance, how deformed dost thou look!"[10]

I encourage you with all my heart to read the documents of the Second Vatican Council as soon as possible. Do not listen to sound bites. Do not rely on fragments of passages taken out of context. Do not uncritically accept the interpretations of those with an ax to grind. Instead, ask the Holy Spirit for wisdom and guidance—and go to the source.

The Council of the Age

"The Second Vatican Council was in peril from its period, which was man-centered, sociologically minded, and spiritually 'horizontal.'"[11] These words from the Dominican scholar Aidan Nichols lucidly capture the third and final component of the paracouncil's rise. The 1960s and '70s were a turbulent time in world history. A passing survey of events in the United States is sufficient to prove it: the sexual revolution, the assassination of John F. Kennedy, Woodstock, the Vietnam War, the Cold War. In short, the years immediately following Vatican II were characterized by a spirit of freelance experimentation, rebellion against authority, rejection of tradition, political upheaval, tense international relationships, and rapid technological development.

This mentality of seeking novelty, trying out new structures, and redefining previously accepted norms certainly bolstered the widespread acceptance of paraconciliar thinking. In an age when doing unconventional things was heroic and casting off the shackles of antiquity was a virtue, certain theologians' interpretations of the Second Vatican Council appeared to be yet another way of "sticking it to the man." People began to see Vatican II as a signal that even the Church was ready to change. No wonder the paracouncil's agenda was welcomed in so many quarters, coinciding as it did with the spirit of the age.

Fueled by the unbridled enthusiasm of the day, those with various social and political agendas found it all too easy to appropriate the conciliar event, leading to a severe reductionism on multiple levels. The Church's rich social justice ministry became mere activism. Her intellectual tradition was traded for subjective sentimentalism. Her sacred worship turned into a communal service of the people and by the people. Slowly but surely, the influence of theologians and clergy promoting the paracouncil became a kind of subculture within the Church until finally, their mentalities, opinions, and paradigms became the mainstream interpretation of Vatican II.

The Conservative Reaction to the Paracouncil

When Sir Isaac Newton said, "For every action there is an equal and opposite reaction," he was talking about physics. But his words apply just as well to our discussion of the council and paracouncil. Though the paracouncil came to dominate popular perceptions of Vatican II, it was not greeted with universal enthusiasm. Now we will take into consideration the "equal and opposite" reaction brought forth by the paracouncil.

On November 1, 1970, a French prelate named Archbishop Marcel Lefebvre founded a new religious organization for priests called the Society of Saint Pius X (SSPX). Although he had affirmed and signed all the major documents of Vatican II, Archbishop Lefebvre was deeply disturbed by the way the work of the council was being interpreted and applied. Specifically, he was stunned by the improvisations and experimentations being inserted into the sacred liturgy, as well as the increasingly unorthodox formation of seminarians. He wrote in one of his letters that "at this moment in time [1969] my most urgent duty is to train priests. . . . I am also convinced that it is the holiness of the priesthood that will save us."[12] Accordingly, the purpose of his new society was "the priesthood and all that pertains to it. . . . The Society must therefore orient the priest towards—and have him concretize in his daily life what is essentially his *raison d'être*: the Holy Sacrifice of the Mass, with all that it means. All that flows from it, and all that complements it."[13]

The SSPX began as a canonically approved endeavor under the jurisdiction of Bishop François Charrière in Switzerland. The society aspired to preserve the dignity of priesthood and renew liturgical devotion. However, due to a number of factors, not least of which was the paracouncil's disparaging attitude toward Catholic tradition, relations between the SSPX and the Church became increasingly strained. By the 1980s, liturgical and doctrinal abuses were widespread throughout many dioceses, especially among members of the clergy. In response to this crisis, St. John Paul II published an apostolic letter on December 4, 1988, outlining malpractices and calling for a return to the true intention of Vatican II's liturgical reform:

> It must be recognized that the application of the liturgical reform has met with difficulties. . . . On occasion there have been noted illicit omissions or additions, rites invented outside the framework of established norms; postures or songs which are not conducive to faith or to a sense of the sacred; abuses in the practice of general absolution; confusion between the ministerial priesthood . . . and the common priesthood of the faithful. . . . It cannot be tolerated that certain priests should take upon themselves the right to compose Eucharistic Prayers or to substitute profane readings for texts from Sacred Scripture. Initiatives of this sort, far from being linked with the liturgical reform as such, or with the books which have issued from it, are in direct contradiction to it, disfigure it and deprive the Christian people of the genuine treasures of the Liturgy of the Church.[14]

Unfortunately, in the eyes of the SSPX, the pope's admonition was too little too late. On June 30 of that same year, Archbishop Lefebvre ordained four bishops without approval from the Holy

See, a deed expressly contradicting the law of the Catholic Church. For Lefebvre, the ordination was a necessary action for maintaining tradition and protecting Catholicism against "conciliar bishops" who, with "doubtful intentions, confer doubtful sacraments."[15] This action also ensured that seminarians in the SSPX would be formed and ordained by bishops sympathetic to Lefebvre's cause. This incurred an automatic excommunication of the four newly ordained bishops as well as Lefebvre himself, effectively putting the group out of communion with the Catholic Church. Pope Benedict XVI remitted the excommunications on January 21, 2009, but the group's status vis-à-vis communion with the Church remains troubled.

Lefebvre was not alone in his concerns. All around the world, clergy and laity alike sought a return to tradition as a means of coping with the changes spreading throughout the Church under the paracouncil's influence. In the United States, groups such as the Catholic Traditionalist Movement (CTM), founded by Fr. Gommar A. De Pauw in 1965, sought to reinforce the traditions being pushed aside by the paracouncil, specifically those pertaining to the sacred liturgy. We will discuss the fallacies involved in these responses in chapter 3. For now, suffice it to say that many of the issues raised by traditionalist groups—especially in regard to the liturgy—are not contentions with the council itself but rather with the ways in which specific individuals promoted paraconciliar opinions.

It was not just problems with the liturgy that led to a defensive reaction among traditionalist Catholics. There were (and still are) a number of other concerns. Moyra Doorly and Fr. Aidan Nichols provide a solid summary in their excellent book-length dialogue, *The Council in Question*:

> [L]iturgical abuses and ecumenical excesses, the widespread return to the lay state of Religious and priests, the catechetical confusion, the obfuscation of the distinction between Christian humanism and civil humanism,

> and the egregious doctrinal deviations which, too often,
> sheltered behind appeal to the "Conciliar spirit," were in
> no way intended by the Council fathers. . . . The move-
> ment called Catholic Traditionalism, or, less graciously,
> Lefebvrism, arose in sharp reaction to the post-conciliar
> crisis. It is a defensive reaction that wished and wishes
> to call a halt to . . . the "decomposition of Catholicism."[16]

Catholic traditionalism is not so much a rebellion as it is a scream—the kind one gives when frustrated at things gone wrong. Whether you agree or disagree with the method, we must admit that the concerns of traditionalists are directed at legitimately problematic trends and realities in the Church today. Why is it that so many Catholics have left the Church in the past fifty years—nearly thirty million in the United States alone? And why is it that those who remain within the Church are often uncatechized in the most basic aspects of the faith? This is a disheartening and sometimes infuriating situation for practicing Catholics, especially young adults and parents trying to raise wholesome Christian families. In their battle against the constant influences of the secular world, many Catholics are experiencing a shortage of the necessary resources for spiritual enrichment, intellectual development, and liturgical piety. These men and women feel alone in their endeavor for sainthood. In frustration, their hearts grow nostalgic for a bygone age. Atheism, materialism, scientism, technology—these things have sucked the air dry, and our young Catholics are gasping for something substantial and profound to breathe in. Traditionalism claims it can fill the void.

Some traditionalists are radical in their opinions and uncharitable in their accusations against so-called Vatican II Catholics (often denounced as "neo-Catholics" or "Novus Ordo Catholics"). But the majority of traditional Catholics I have encountered are simply people, often young people, who are discouraged by the overall lack of spirituality, beauty, and depth provided at their local parish or diocese. They do not run to traditionalism because it is their first choice, but because nothing better has been shown to them.

The teachings of Vatican II are saturated with sacred scripture and sacred tradition. Yet, many of those implementing the council on the grassroots level failed to allow this brilliance to shine, preferring instead teachings or initiatives that coincided with their own theological preferences. This has left a lot of Catholics with a bad taste in their mouths for Vatican II as they associate their lackluster (or outright unorthodox) experience of Catholicism with the council itself. This distaste is reinforced by popular traditionalist commentators whose message of Vatican II's supposed errors resonates with disillusioned Catholics.

Dealing with Disappointment in the Church

It is valuable at this point to offer a brief reflection on how to deal with disappointment in the shortcomings of the Church. This is important, because some traditionalists' concerns are legitimate—for example, the need to regain solemnity and tradition in the sacred liturgy. However, their sheer frustration with the current situation in the Church sometimes leads to a visceral, overly forceful presentation of these concerns, making their claims unappealing. As a result, the relationship between traditional Catholics and others inside the Church has become increasingly aggravated. Likewise, traditionalists' rhetoric often causes people already wary of tradition to see it as increasingly objectionable. Over time, this can lead to deep-seated bitterness on both sides, crippling any efforts toward reconciliation.

I deal with this on a regular basis as a parish priest. I have frequent conversations with young traditionalists who are at the point of abandoning their local parish. They despair because, in their eyes, everything seems to be going wrong. The preaching is lukewarm, the liturgies are irreverent, and the catechesis is shoddy. Yet, when they try to speak to their pastors and fellow parishioners about these issues, they are rejected, belittled, or written off as trad-Catholics. Entering into a respectful and open dialogue with traditional Catholics is an important pastoral issue not often addressed. That being said, abandoning our local parish or becoming hypercritical of the Church is never the answer.

If we are to effect true reform in the heart of Mother Church, it will be as her children, not as her critics. It will be in humility, not severity. There will always be problems in the Church. But the answer is not to leave her or stone her, but to suffer these shortcomings within her arms. St. Paul exemplifies this virtue beautifully in his words to the Colossians: "I rejoice in my sufferings for your sake, and in my flesh I am filling up what is lacking in the afflictions of Christ on behalf of his body, which is the Church" (Col 1:24). Likewise, in his letter to the struggling church of Galatia, we hear the apostle cry out, "My children, for whom I am again in labor until Christ be formed in you!" (Gal 4:19).

Pope Francis calls every Christian to embody the compassion of St. Paul through an "art of accompaniment."[17] As baptized persons, we are tasked with maintaining a patient endurance within the brokenness of the world, meeting each person where they are while simultaneously summoning them to where they ought to be. This evangelical disposition applies not only to our service of other human beings, but also to our obedience to the Church. Although we should be honest in assessing areas for continued growth, we must also be vigilant against harboring bitterness or resentment when reform does not happen as quickly or radically as we would like.

This requires a profound faith in the Holy Spirit, trusting that he is constantly at work within the Body of Christ even when it seems otherwise. At the same time, it calls us to an enduring love that does not lose hope as it sees past the failings of the Church into the very core of her being, which remains safeguarded by the Father.

This is not to dismiss the need for improvement, but rather to provide an alternative to the prevailing sentiments of frustration, anger, and callousness that some traditionalists harbor toward the Church. I've encountered traditionalists who refuse to admit that Vatican II did anything right and who insist that any priest or bishop who disagrees with their ideas is heretical. However, there are many more traditionalists who *want* to participate in the life of their home parish. They are just waiting for a reason to come back.

The good news is that if we can reclaim Vatican II—the true council in all its fullness—we can find a path to greater unity. Renewed obedience to what the council teaches about liturgy (not to mention architecture, tradition, sacred music, the Bible, Catholic education, and evangelization) will prove vital in bridging the divide between traditionalists and local parish communities. Some claim that Vatican II is the great divider in the Church. In reality, it ought to be the very thing that bridges the divide.

2

THE TRUE SPIRIT OF VATICAN II

Now that we've delineated the origins and consequences of the paracouncil, we must seek to understand the true spirit of Vatican II.

Understanding Development in Church Teaching

Correcting the skewed applications of a council is nothing new in Church history. It was for this reason, immediately following the Council of Ephesus in AD 431, that St. Vincent of Lérins penned his *Commonitory*, a book dedicated to explaining the development of Christian dogma while providing guidelines for the proper interpretation of conciliar teachings. His description of upheaval after the Council of Ephesus is eerily familiar. On the one hand, St. Vincent identifies a group of theologians who were seeking adulterated novelty in Church doctrine by casting off antiquity and promoting personal interpretations of the Catholic faith. In response to these thinkers, the holy bishop exhorts:

> It is our duty not to lead religion whither we would, but rather to follow religion whither it leads; and that it is part of Christian modesty and gravity not to hand down

> our own beliefs or observances to those who come after
> us, but to preserve and keep what we have received from
> those who went before us.[1]

To guard against the "seduction of novelty," St. Vincent quotes St. Jerome, who reaffirms the indispensable nature of sacred tradition in preserving "the precepts of our predecessors and not transgress[ing] with rude rashness the landmarks which we have inherited from them."[2]

On the other hand, St. Vincent is careful to guard against a stagnant traditionalism. While asserting the importance of sacred tradition, he also identifies the need for development in the life of the Church:

> Someone will say perhaps, "Shall there then be no prog-
> ress in Christ's Church?" Certainly; all possible progress.
> For what being is there, so envious of men, so full of
> hatred to God, who would seek to forbid it? Yet, on
> condition that it be real progress, not alteration of the
> faith. . . . For it is right that those ancient doctrines of
> heavenly philosophy should, as time goes on, be cared
> for, smoothed, polished; but not that they should be
> changed, not that they should be maimed, not that they
> shall be mutilated. They may receive proof, illustration,
> definiteness; but they must retain withal their complete-
> ness, their integrity, their characteristic properties. . . .
> This I say, is what the Catholic Church . . . has accom-
> plished by the decrees of her Councils.[3]

In his genius, St. Vincent recognized the necessary tension between tradition and progress in the development of Catholic dogma. Christian doctrine does not exist in the form of discrete propositions, political ideals, or ethical codes, but rather as a dynamic relationship of beliefs.[4] This is because the Church, far from being a mere institution, is a living organism rooted in the life of Christ. She is "built on the foundation of the apostles and prophets" as "the body of Christ," with Christ himself as "the head" (Eph 2:20; 1 Cor 12:28; Col 1:18). Thus, before the Church formulates dogma, dogma is *first and foremost Christ himself being unveiled and encountered anew by the Church*; it is God revealing himself to us and establishing the means of his self-communication.[5]

This is why Christianity is most properly called a "creed" (*symbolum*). *Symbolum* comes from the Greek *symballein*, which means "to bind/throw together." It is a verb. The belief of the Church is not a passive reality or a mere intellectual consent. To profess Catholicism is to be "creed-ed," bound and incorporated into a relationship that is "living and effective" (Heb 4:12). And like every relationship, it must be both remembered (tradition) and enjoyed afresh (renewal).

St. Vincent's appreciation of the need to return to the sources of tradition as well as continually open our hearts to the Holy Spirit's promptings of renewal provides an authentic paradigm by which to understand the teachings of the Second Vatican Council. Vatican II is not a progressive council seeking sheer novelty, nor is it a traditionalist council convened to ossify faith. It is a *Catholic* council, simultaneously inspired by the wisdom of tradition and the impulse of renewal.

There are two words typically employed to denote the council's dedication to both tradition and renewal: *ressourcement* and *aggiornamento*. Fr. Robert P. Imbelli offers an introduction to these terms in his superb book *Rekindling the Christic Imagination*:

> The council, as is well known, undertook its labors under the standards of *ressourcement* and *aggiornamento*. *Ressourcement* indicated the council's effort to rediscover, with fresh eyes, the wellsprings of the faith, in particular the Scriptures themselves and the reception of and reflection upon the Scriptures by early bishops

and theologians of the Church. . . . By *aggiornamento*,
the council indicated its intention to bring the Good
News of Jesus Christ proclaimed by tradition into the
world today, addressing the aspirations and concerns of
contemporary men and women in language that speaks
to them in a way both intelligible and pastoral.[6]

With this summary in mind, we will dive more deeply into these
two terms and see how they contribute to the mission of the Second Vatican Council.

Ressourcement and *Aggiornamento*

Let us begin our discussion with a reflection on sacred scripture.
In Psalm 48 we hear the following words:

Go about Zion, walk all around it,
   note the number of its towers.
Consider the ramparts, examine its citadels,
   that you may tell future generations:
That this is God,
   our God for ever and ever.
   He will lead us until death.
   (lines 13–15)

St. Augustine sees this psalmody as an allusion to the Catholic
Church. It is the Church of Christ that is the new Zion built upon
the holy mountain of Jesus' Passion, Death, and Resurrection.[7]
The first stanza of the psalm ("Go about Zion, walk all around it")
represents the necessity of living from the heart of the Church. As
Christians, we must be fully immersed in Mother Church, sharing in the grace of her sacraments and seeking the depths of her
wisdom.[8] Likewise, we are called to consider every "rampart" of
her doctrine and examine every "citadel" of her tradition. Why?
"To tell future generations: That this is God." In these words, we
see the responsibility of evangelization, the need to present the

wisdom of tradition with renewed vigor to "future generations." St. Augustine's insight on Psalm 48 perfectly embodies the goal of Vatican II. The council strived both to re-source the understanding of Mother Church in the wellspring of her tradition and to find enthusiastic ways to share this tradition with the world.

Tradition and Ressourcement

Nowadays, "tradition" possesses a generally negative connotation. This is true not just among people in the Church, but in society as a whole. The label "traditional" implies close-mindedness, rigidity, and staleness. Unfortunately, these sentiments come from a narrow definition of tradition that sees it as a set of fossilized rules or outdated norms. As such, tradition is typically branded the enemy of progress. But in reality, it is the complete opposite.

The word "tradition" comes from the Latin verb *tradere*, meaning "to hand on" or "to hand over." Originally, it was used in the Roman Empire to denote a legal transaction such as the handing over of a piece of property. Culturally, the term represents the handing over of one generation's wisdom to another. *Tradere* properly understood, therefore, is active, not stagnant. It is something that is happening, not something that has passed. It is a living event, not an inert object. The German composer Gustav Mahler defines it poetically: "Tradition is not the worship of ashes, but the preservation of fire." Tradition is a burning torch lit by our forebears to guide us along the paths of human endeavor. This torch is fueled by the knowledge gleaned from countless mistakes and successes, triumphs and failures, tragedies and achievements.

As human beings, we are the inheritors of an ongoing dialogue, the heirs of a transgenerational conversation. In order to genuinely progress, we must engage in this conversation considering the conclusions of those who went before us and allowing the past to have its say in our future. G. K. Chesterton summarizes the point with his usual wit: "Tradition means giving votes to the most obscure of all classes, our ancestors. It is the democracy of the dead. Tradition refuses to submit to the small and arrogant oligarchy of those who merely happen to be walking about."[9] We are not monads or creatures in isolation. Our civilization stands on the shoulders of our ancestors. To attempt progress without the light of tradition is to stumble about in the dark.

Tradition, "taken in its basic, exact and completely general sense . . . is the very principle of the whole" Christian experience.[10] St. John the Evangelist portrays this beautifully in chapter 19 of his gospel:

> There was a vessel filled with common wine. So they put a sponge soaked in wine on a sprig of hyssop and put it up to his mouth. When Jesus had taken the wine, he said, "It is finished." And bowing his head, he handed over (*tradidit*) the spirit. (Jn 19:29–30)

On the Cross, Jesus handed over his spirit of trusting obedience and love to the Father. This handing over of his spirit to the Father at Golgotha is the original "tradition"—the act from which all Catholic tradition flows. What is more, this handing over is infused with the flesh of *our* humanity. "He was pierced for our sins" and "bore our sins in his body upon the cross, so that, free from sin, we might live for righteousness" as "children of God, and if children, heirs, heirs of God" (Is 53:5; 1 Pt 2:24; Rom 8:16–17).

Thus, Catholic tradition is sourced in divine tradition. It is rooted in the divine handing over of the Son to the Father. This tradition between Jesus and the Father constitutes the basis of Christianity. Jesus gives us to the Father through himself and through himself gives us the Father. This is why he came, so that he might return to the Father (see John 14:28 and 16:28) and in so doing make us one with the Father as he and the Father are one (see John 17:21). For this reason, Christ imbues divine tradition

within the very infrastructure of the Church, as reflected in the
Eucharistic Prayer:

> Take this, all of you and eat of it
> For this is my Body
> which will be given up (*tradetur*) for you.

The Eucharist is Jesus making divine tradition ever-present to the
Church. The sacrifice of the Holy Mass constitutes the epicenter
of tradition; it is the reality that essentially shapes the Church's
spirituality and identity.[11] Tradition in its fullest sense, then, is
the Church's active participation in the handing over of the Son to
the Father, an offering established "once for all" on behalf of those
who "are being consecrated" (see Hebrews 10:1–18). No words
capture this reality more perfectly than that stirring acclamation
proclaimed at the high point of the Eucharistic Prayer:

> Through him and with him and in him, O God almighty
> Father, in the unity of the Holy Spirit, all glory and
> honor is yours forever and ever. Amen.

The apostles were entrusted with this tradition by Christ himself. They constantly reflected on it, contemplated it, preached it,
and lived it. John wrote of it as an "eyewitness" whose "testimony is
true" (Jn 19:35), and Paul exhorted his converts to hold fast to it no
matter the consequences (see 1 Cor 11:2; 2 Thes 2:15). Throughout
the ages, this tradition was passed on from heart to heart, with each
generation seeking to preserve its dignity and suffuse its profundity
in the souls of others. Every liturgical practice, song, art piece, poem,
law, building—all of these are inspired by the tradition of Christ's
sacrifice to the Father. God himself is the origin of Catholic tradition.

Why am I going to such great lengths to properly define tradition? For the same reason I am writing this book—to reclaim
tradition from the extremes. Since the Second Vatican Council,
both paraconciliar and traditionalist thinkers have diminished

the meaning of tradition. On the one hand, paraconciliar thought rejects tradition wholesale in lieu of personal ideologies. Tradition, according to the paracouncil, is a threat to progress in the Church and is extraneous to the needs of modern times. This kind of thinking was popularized during the 1970s and '80s, leading to an abandonment of many treasured beliefs and practices in Catholicism.

On the other hand, as a reaction to the paracouncil, a large number of Catholics reject anything promoted by Vatican II, clinging to the rubrics of past liturgies or traditional religious practices. This reaction has two negatives effects. First, it reduces tradition to little more than a set of rules or rote norms confined to a particular time in Church history. Such a deficient notion of tradition leads to the supposition that a simple return to pre–Vatican II practices will solve the problems in the Church, which is most certainly not the case. Second, it results in the ossification of tradition. By this I mean that tradition is no longer seen as a dynamic activity being realized by Jesus Christ right now in the life of the Church, and devolves into a relic of the past. An adequate understanding of tradition is essential if we are to safeguard ourselves against the ossification of religion. Tradition and traditionalism are two very different things. One is living and effective, the other is dead and stale.

Through *ressourcement* (literally, "a return to the sources"), the council sought to integrate sacred scripture and the theology of the ancient Church Fathers into the common life of the faithful. This is one of the main missions of Vatican II. In regard to the study of sacred scripture, numerous advancements had been made since the Council of Trent (1545–1563). These advances were prompted by a series of landmark discoveries in the eighteenth, nineteenth, and twentieth centuries. In the mid-1800s, for example, scholars rummaging through the library of an Egyptian monastery found a Bible dating from the fourth century AD. Dubbed the "Sinai

Bible" (Codex Sinaiticus), it is now recognized as one of the oldest Bibles in existence. And in 1946, a group of Bedouin shepherds found several jars filled with aged papyri. Later called the Dead Sea Scrolls, these texts remain one of the great religious finds of recent history. Discoveries such as these proved valuable tools, serving as instruments for comparative studies as well as benchmarks for evaluating the evolution of literary style and language.

The Church responded to these discoveries with enthusiasm. Pope Leo XIII published an encyclical in 1893 authorizing the use of newly formulated research techniques in biblical scholarship. Sixteen years later, Pope St. Pius X founded the Pontifical Biblical Institute, a postgraduate facility dedicated to studying sacred scripture. Finally, on September 30, 1943, Pope Pius XII issued *Divino afflante Spiritu* ("Inspired by the Holy Spirit"), a letter endorsing the use of various scholarly methods in Catholic Bible study. There was also one other important decision made by Pope Pius XII. Typically, St. Jerome's Latin Vulgate provided the basis for translations of Catholic Bibles into other languages. Now, however, it was the original languages of the biblical texts (Hebrew, Aramaic, and Greek) that should be used when translating sacred scripture into the vernacular.

Biblical scholarship was not the only area to experience growth in the post-Tridentine period. Patristics (the study of ancient Christian writers and theologians) also thrived. For instance, the *Didache*—a text from the first century AD detailing early Christian beliefs—is one of the most ancient Catholic works besides the New Testament. Although the *Didache* is mentioned in several manuscripts, including St. Eusebius's *Ecclesiastical History* (ca. AD 312–324), a transcription of the text was not found until 1875. The discovery of many such texts gave unprecedented insights into the teachings of nascent Catholicism.

A renaissance in the field of theology ensued. These discoveries were akin to the opening of a time capsule, reintroducing the Church to the intuition and genius of her first children. Furthermore, great strides were made in printing and disseminating patristic texts throughout the eighteenth and nineteenth centuries, the most notable being Fr. Jacques-Paul Migne's herculean accomplishment of editing and compiling more than three hundred volumes of early Church documents in both Greek and Latin! Writings hitherto unknown were now accessible to a wide audience. The homilies of St. John Chrysostom, the catechesis of St. Cyril of Jerusalem, the sacramental teachings of St. Basil the Great, the commentaries of Origen—thousands of pages of ancient texts were now available for reading and study. Theologians such as Johann Adam Möhler (1796–1838), Matthias Joseph Scheeben (1835–1888), and St. John Henry Newman (1801–1890) seamlessly integrated the wisdom of the Church Fathers into their theological writings, reviving Catholic scholarship. This was especially true in regard to ecclesiology (the study of the Church) and Mariology (the study of the Blessed Virgin Mary). These two fields of study became incredibly influential for the Second Vatican Council, specifically its document on the Church (*Lumen Gentium*).

    Ressourcement was Vatican II's way of encouraging Christians, lay and ordained alike, to "consider the ramparts" and "examine the citadels" of our Catholic faith (Ps 48:13). The council fervently attempted to source itself in the Church's tradition. We can see this in the construction of the council's documents themselves. There are more than 125 references to ancient Church Fathers in the four major constitutions alone! St. Thomas Aquinas, St. Bonaventure, and Gratian also make several appearances. Previous ecumenical councils are alluded to frequently, including the Councils of Nicaea, Chalcedon, Ephesus, Orange, Florence, and Trent. The teachings of several popes are likewise mentioned: St. Pius X, Pius XII, Benedict XV, and Leo XIII. All this gives credence to the fact that Vatican II was an ecumenical council firmly rooted in sacred tradition.

The council reasoned that a more profound appreciation of sacred scripture accompanied by a reintroduction of patristic teachings in the wider Church would both deepen the faith of God's people and equip the faithful to inspire and convert the modern world. This hope to inspire and convert the modern world leads to our next point of discussion.

Renewal and Aggiornamento

Aggiornamento is an Italian word that means "bring up to date." It was popularized by St. John XXIII, who used the word in a speech he offered on the Feast of the Conversion of St. Paul, January 25, 1959, at the Basilica of St. Paul Outside the Walls in Rome. The date and place were not coincidental. St. Paul's conversion is among the most important feasts in all Christendom. It is a day on which we celebrate the gift of the Church's greatest evangelist.

Paul was a man of evangelical genius. With tireless zeal he preached the Gospel "whether it is convenient or inconvenient" so that salvation might be brought to those beyond "the lost sheep of the house of Israel" (2 Tm 4:2; Mt 15:24). He also possessed a keen pastoral sensibility as demonstrated in his interaction with the Athenians at the Areopagus:

> Then Paul stood up at the Areopagus and said: "You Athenians, I see that in every respect you are very religious. For as I walked around looking carefully at your shrines, I even discovered an altar inscribed, 'To an Unknown God.' What therefore you unknowingly worship, I proclaim to you. The God who made the world and all that is in it." (Acts 17:22–24)

Misguided as the Athenians' worship may have been, Paul recognized the inherent goodness of their culture and their inclination toward the truth. He utilized this insight in preaching to the

Athenians about the salvation of Christ. With this example from the life of St. Paul in mind, the pope's usage of *aggiornamento* becomes clearer.

By introducing the notion of *aggiornamento* against the backdrop of the feast of St. Paul's conversion, the pope associates the term with the evangelical zeal of the great "apostle to the Gentiles" (Rom 11:13). In so doing, St. John XXIII protects *aggiornamento* from being reduced to a mere progressivist ideology or anti-traditionalism. He is not simply calling for the Church to be modernized or to "get hip with the times." It is much deeper than that. St. John XXIII is inviting the People of God to follow St. Paul's example and awaken a passion for preaching the Gospel through a renewed encounter with the tradition of the Church. *Aggiornamento* therefore presupposes *ressourcement*. You cannot have one without the other: "Without the compliment of *aggiornamento*, *ressourcement* risks becoming mere antiquarianism: a museum tour through ancient artifacts. Without *ressourcement*, *aggiornamento* can easily slip into a cultural accommodation that lacks substance."[12]

My father is a water-well contractor. Growing up, my brothers and I used to help him at the drilling rig. We would run the hydraulics and dig drain ditches while he latched galvanized piping to the drill bit. It was grueling work. Depending on the depth and location of the well, it could take hours to reach water. Some wells needed to tap into the Floridan aquifer, one of the largest water systems in the United States. Breaching the aquifer remains one of the most impressive and formative experiences of my childhood. There are few feelings more invigorating than seeing sediment and muck give way to freshwater.

One time in particular, I remember penetrating an artesian aquifer, which is part of the aquifer under a superabundant amount of positive pressure. As soon as we pierced the limestone, water came spewing out of the drill hole, spraying thirty feet into the air. It was amazing. Water that had been trapped underground for more than twenty thousand years filled the drilling area. We looked upward and opened our mouths as ice-cold water fell from the sky. The water was fresh and tasted better than anything you could buy at the store. Our overheated bodies, covered in sweat and mud, were washed clean, leaving us refreshed and renewed. This water was the incomparable best of Mother Nature's produce.

My childhood experience of drilling a well is analogous to the relationship between *ressourcement* and *aggiornamento*. *Ressourcement* is the drilling rig. Through the guidance of the Holy Spirit, theologians plumb the depths of the Church's history, sifting through the sediment and minerals of ancient resources. Their goal is to tap into the artesian aquifer of sacred tradition and sacred scripture, a source of superabundant wisdom and holiness. This drilling takes centuries of discovery, research, and debate. But, eventually, the workers puncture through the barrier, releasing a torrent of insight inspired by the early Church Fathers and the Bible. Yet, the purpose of this endeavor is not merely to breach wisdom, just as the purpose of drilling is not simply to penetrate the aquifer. Rather, a well only reaches its proper end when we drink from it, when it provides sustenance and irrigation.

In the same way, the purpose of *ressourcement* is not to reserve newly appreciated teachings for academics or scholars alone, but rather to break open the springhead of antiquity so that it can seep into the very life of Mother Church, saturating God's people with refreshing waters. This is *aggiornamento*, to drink deeply from the artesian aquifer of sacred tradition and sacred scripture. *Aggiornamento* is to enjoy the work of *ressourcement*, to relish that which was buried under the ground of time as it shoots to the surface of the present age. At the same time, it is not a simple re-presentation of bygone ideas. Rather, *aggiornamento* speaks to the Church's mission to transmit eternal truths in new ways that speak to the needs of the current world. This is the whole mission of Vatican II.

For the past several centuries, the Holy Spirit has unearthed countless springs of knowledge for Mother Church. Not since the apostolic age have Catholics been afforded such opportunities to encounter the thought and teachings of their ancestors. Never before have so many writings and texts been translated into the vernacular and provided for study among the faithful. Yet, how little the average Catholic drinks of this fountain! The Second Vatican Council has given us everything we need to set our families and parishes on fire. If we read the documents, study the sources, contemplate the spirituality, and practice *accurately* the teachings of Vatican II, we will experience a restoration and renewal of the faith.

The Style and Logic of Vatican II

Vatican II represents a major pivot in evangelical and theological style. Whereas in the preceding several centuries the Church was defined by a more *scholastic* style, Vatican II shifted the Church's way of teaching to a more *catechetical* style. For an example, let's look at the difference between the *Baltimore Catechism* (1885) and the *Catechism of the Catholic Church* (1992). The first statement of the *Baltimore Catechism* reads as follows:

> Q: Who made us?
> A: God made us.

That's it—short, sweet, and to the point. The *Catechism of the Catholic Church*, on the other hand, has this as its opening statement:

> God, infinitely perfect and blessed in himself, in a plan
> of sheer goodness freely created man to make him share
> in his own blessed life. For this reason, at every time
> and in every place, God draws close to man. He calls

> man to seek him, to know him, to love him with all
> his strength. He calls together all men, scattered and
> divided by sin, into the unity of his family, the Church.
> To accomplish this, when the fullness of time had come,
> God sent his Son as Redeemer and Savior. In his Son
> and through him, he invites men to become, in the Holy
> Spirit, his adopted children and thus heirs of his blessed
> life. (*CCC*, 1)

Big difference. The *Baltimore Catechism* is similar in style to the writings of St. Thomas Aquinas. It favors brevity and conciseness. The *Catechism of the Catholic Church*, however, prefers an organic and gradual presentation of the faith. This is not to say it is "better" than the *Baltimore Catechism*. It is not a matter of better or worse, but of mission and purpose. The *Baltimore Catechism* is valuable for its encapsulation of the basic tenets of the faith, and it's geared toward rote memorization. T*he Catechism of the Catholic Church*, on the other hand, provides more nuanced theological reflection. The example above is representative of Vatican II's style as a whole—and it's reflective of the style found in the ancient commentaries and writings of the Church Fathers. The conciliar documents read like spiritual works, weaving in and out of various theological reflections and gradually unveiling the truth of the Gospel.

This was an important change to make. The modern world is accustomed to scientific clarity and exacting calculations—and sometimes these come at the expense of beauty and depth. The council fathers, inspired by the ancient Church, present dogma, doctrine, and theology with a refreshing liveliness. Instead of merely stating a fact, they mine it and let us examine every precious gem.

This is not to say that the scholastic style of presentation is bad. Different periods in Church history demand different techniques of evangelization. In the world of Christendom, one could present the faith in a scholastic way because the basic tenants of the faith saturated culture. In our current post-Christian world, however, the faith can no longer be taken for granted. There needs to be a re-presentation of Catholicism. Our current society is unfamiliar with even the simplest aspects of Christianity. Although this is tragic in one sense, it is also an opportunity. Like the first disciples of Jesus, our generation is speaking to a world that sees Catholicism as something novel and strange. This is especially true of millennials and Gen Z. The Holy Spirit through the Second Vatican Council recognized this reality and gave the Church the necessary approach to catechize our own time.

Some people say that Vatican II is a pastoral council. But this misses the mark. More than anything, Vatican II is a kerygmatic council. The Greek word *kerygma* means "preaching." It is a prophetic term indicating the proclamation of a much-needed message. For Christians, the word *kerygma* refers to the original content of the Christian message, those fundamental principles of the Catholic faith. It also denotes that initial zeal and ingenuity with which the early Church proclaimed the Gospel. Vatican II, therefore, seeks to guide the faithful in a renewal of what C. S. Lewis calls "mere Christianity," those foundational aspects of Christ and his Church. Its whole purpose is to reconnect God's people with the heart of Catholicism—the joyful, vital proclamation of the Gospel as recorded in sacred scripture and unfolded by the Fathers of the Church.

This style is providential considering the order of the four major council documents. They begin with the sacred liturgy (*Sacrosanctum Concilium*), for it is the liturgy that nourishes and sustains the Church. The liturgy is her central activity and most important responsibility, the wellspring from which the Church's identity flows (*Lumen Gentium*). The Church is directed by the grace of divine revelation (*Dei Verbum*), as shown forth through sacred tradition and sacred scripture. Finally, under the guiding

hands of divine revelation she is able to evangelize the modern
world (*Gaudium et Spes*).

I call this ordering of the documents the "logic of Vatican II,"
meaning, the way the council thinks. The image below illustrates
this logic:

To really appreciate the four major documents, we must see them
in relation to one another. Doing so reveals not only the logic of
the council, but indeed the basic logic of Christianity. Our lives are
sourced in the liturgy before all else as we receive the grace of the
sacraments. This in turn makes us living members of the Church.
In the arms of Mother Church, we are formed by the wisdom of
sacred scripture and sacred tradition. Then, after adequate formation, we are asked to go out into the world to preach the Gospel.
Any time our theology is off-kilter or our spirituality gets out of
whack, it is because we have failed in some way to respect this
basic logic of Christian life. Some of us go out to preach without
proper study and prayer. Others prioritize studying the Bible but
do not go to Mass regularly. There are many ways to disorder our

priorities, but the results remain the same: a Christian life that is not being lived to the fullest.

I felt it was only fitting that I attempt to write this book with the style and logic of Vatican II. Rather than simply quoting a document and giving a straight answer on what it means, I lean toward elaborating, meditating, and theologizing on key themes, drawing not just our minds, but hopefully our hearts and souls to the council's essential insights and intentions. My hope is that as you read, you will begin to experience what I've felt in my own heart—a deep appreciation for Vatican II's profound beauty, spiritual richness, and power to renew the way we live as the Church.

Many of us ask, "Lord, what do you want me to do with my life? How am I supposed to serve you? What is your will?" These are questions that can only be answered if we are thinking and praying from *within* the heart of the Church. It is impossible to know our vocation outside the Body of Christ. It is only when we are thinking with her, praying with her, living with her that the mystery of our own existence gradually unfolds before us. So it has been in my own life. Discovering and embracing the vision of Vatican II oriented my soul to God's will, showing me that the Spirit is actively working in the Church and that he is inviting me to do the same.

As I studied the council documents and sought to conform my mind to the wisdom of the Church, they gave me a sense of direction and made my mission clear: I am called to become a saint by living out the joy, wisdom, and hope of the Second Vatican Council. I must immerse myself in the solemnity and dignity of the sacred liturgy, be formed by the loving embrace of the Church, contemplate sacred scripture, and uphold sacred tradition so as to preach the Gospel to a world very much in need of its healing mercy.

This is not my mission alone. It is one entrusted to our whole generation. Each of us in our own capacity and utilizing our unique talents is being asked by God to re-evangelize the world, not just for ourselves but for our children and grandchildren. For my part, I know I will not live to see the full fruits of my labor. And that is fine: "For here the saying is verified that 'One sows and another reaps.' I sent you to reap what you have not worked for; others have done the work, and you are sharing the fruits of their work" (Jn 4:37–38). My prayer is that our generation of Catholics will plant, tend, and protect the vineyard given us by Vatican II. If we do, we will have the great joy of seeing others being sanctified by the fruits of our work.

3

THE SACRED LITURGY

It's no coincidence that the first document published by the Second Vatican Council was its Constitution on the Sacred Liturgy, entitled *Sacrosanctum Concilium*. The prioritization of this document reveals a deep spiritual truth about the place of worship in Christian living, namely, that *adoring and glorifying God comes before all else*. If the Church cannot celebrate the liturgy faithfully and reverently, then all her other tasks will fall short.

St. Benedict keenly summarizes this reality in his famous Rule: *Operi Dei nihil praeponatur* ("Nothing is to be preferred to the Work of God").[1] When St. Benedict refers to the "Work of God," he is not talking about writing, preaching, or social justice. In the strictest sense, God's work is the sacred liturgy.

We encounter God most intimately in and through worship. Adoring God is the context in which we receive from him the guiding principles of our mission in the world. For this reason, Vatican II describes the sacred liturgy as the "source and summit" of the Church's life (*SSC*, 10). In other words, the liturgy is not just one activity among many. Rather, it is "a sacred action surpassing all others. No other action of the Church can equal its efficacy by the same title and to the same degree."

Unfortunately, the council's emphasis on the primacy of the sacred liturgy is often muted by both its supporters and its critics.

Among those who applaud Vatican II, I've observed an inclination to focus on the council's pastoral component while overlooking its theological and spiritual foundations. In a society overcome by activism and busyness, it is a temptation among some within the Church to stress social justice or evangelization in lieu of worship, prayer, and contemplation. As a result, we frequently hear how the council encourages us to dialogue with other Christian denominations or work toward economic fairness, but we rarely hear about the council's teachings on the importance of beautiful architecture in the construction of church buildings or the obligation of pastors to educate the faithful in Gregorian chant.

Conversely, those who regard Vatican II with suspicion generally accept the notion that the council banalized the sacred liturgy. This is mostly based on negative experiences Catholics suffered as a result of paraconciliar ideologies in the years immediately following the council. Clergy often failed to sufficiently catechize the faithful about liturgical reforms. Even worse, many things introduced or suppressed in the name of Vatican II were in fact never addressed by the council. Overnight, people who were accustomed to celebrating Mass in Latin and *ad orientem* showed up for the Sunday service to find the high altar ripped out of the wall, statues removed from the sanctuary, and the priest praying the liturgy in English while facing the people.

I frequently ask my older parishioners to share their memories of this transition, and several common themes emerge from their recollections. All of them agree that it was a jarring, even shocking, experience. Most did not understand why these modifications were taking place and felt as if their Catholic heritage was being erased. When questioned about the changes, their priests often insisted it was what Vatican II wanted. They remember hearing homilies about the need to get rid of "old Church" mentalities and start Catholicism anew. Some recall priests publicly shaming parishioners who desired to receive Communion kneeling or on the tongue, even though Vatican II does not forbid either of these practices!

In the wake of these kinds of experiences, a number of people left the Catholic Church and started attending SSPX parishes or other traditionalist sects. In my opinion, the mishandling of Vatican II's teachings is one of the main reasons the SSPX and other traditionalist movements continue to be successful today. I truly believe that if we reclaim Vatican II and its authentic vision for the sacred liturgy, the gap between Catholicism and those who find themselves drawn toward traditionalist movements can be bridged.

Now, it would be unfair to characterize all the clergy, religious, and lay leaders of the post-conciliar period as intentionally misrepresenting Vatican II. In reality, most people who sought reform did so with goodwill and a genuine wish to promote what they believed to be Vatican II's initiatives. However, due to the influence of the paracouncil, specifically through the assertions of certain theologians and the media, many diocesan and parochial leaders were misinformed about the Second Vatican Council and found themselves implementing someone else's interpretation of Vatican II as opposed to what the documents actually instructed.

Furthermore, the influence of secular mentalities within the Church has led to an unfortunate politicization of the liturgy. Certain functions and traditions are now designated as "liberal" or "conservative." For example, if a person prefers the Mass to be celebrated in Latin, they are labeled a conservative Catholic and de facto hater of Vatican II, whereas someone who listens to praise-and-worship music is more liberal and assumed to be in sync with the spirit of Vatican II. These kinds of generalized, politically charged assumptions impede rational and constructive conversation about liturgy, thus crippling our ability to provide much-needed formation of the faithful. Thankfully, the Second Vatican Council gives us the tools necessary to overcome these political hurdles.

If your primary impressions about Vatican II's teachings on the liturgy are based on the polarized discussions prominent in the Church today—especially on social media—you might be surprised to hear that Vatican II did not simply provide a list of changes or new laws for how the liturgy should be practiced. Instead, the council fathers shaped their commentary on the liturgy with edifying reflections on tradition and scripture. In so doing, the council reveals how its teachings are in continuity with the Catholic faith while simultaneously placing its reforms within a larger theological framework. Thus, the council fathers show, by way of catechesis, that the changes encouraged by Vatican II are not a matter of liturgical preference or ideology. Rather, they represent the Church's ongoing mission to promote the Gospel afresh to each generation by building on the wisdom of ages past. As such, in keeping with their initiative to "impart an ever-increasing vigor to the Christian life of the faithful," the council fathers provide an inspiring synthesis of the Catholic faith, not only in the document on the liturgy but indeed in all of the council's major documents (*SSC* 1).

Support for liturgical reform was not a passing whim or spur-of-the-moment decision. The century leading up to Vatican II had seen a revival in the field of liturgical theology owing especially to the rediscovery and translation of patristic texts as well as an increased interest in biblical studies among both Catholic and Protestant scholars. The ancient Church's understanding of the sacred liturgy inspired a series of liturgical reforms years before the Second Vatican Council, including St. Pius X's instruction on sacred music and Pope Pius XII's restructuring of Holy Week. Both of these saintly popes reference ancient Christian practices as inspiration for their reforms.[2]

This academic revival was coupled with a pastoral concern, namely, the general lack of liturgical piety among the faithful. By the nineteenth and twentieth centuries, the average Catholic did not possess an adequate conception of the sacred liturgy or an awareness of their unique role as laity in the life of the Church. Although popular devotions such as the Rosary, Angelus, novenas, and processions were widely practiced before Vatican II, most Catholics lacked a spirituality that flowed from the sacramental life of the Church.

Put more bluntly, a marked separation had developed between the *celebration of* the liturgy—which was seen as the duty of the priest—and the people's *participation in* the liturgy. This is why it was common for people to pray the Rosary or read religious books during Mass until the time for Holy Communion. A reform of the liturgy was much needed! However, the council fathers had no intention of undermining the beauty of the sacred liturgy or its solemnity. They were quite clear in asserting "sound tradition" as the basis of reform, as well as the necessity to safeguard "unchangeable elements divinely instituted" by Christ (*SSC* 4, 21).

The council did not reorder the liturgy out of dislike for previous forms of celebration, but rather for the sake of instilling a greater sense of familiarity among the People of God. The faithful need to know what the liturgy is at its core and why it is irreplaceable in the history of salvation. The council fathers summarized this ideal with the phrase "active participation"—a concept we will explore later in the chapter.

Following the council's lead, we will not immediately jump to points of contention brought on by conciliar reforms. Rather, I will provide a spiritual reflection about the liturgy based on the writings of Vatican II and its principle of active participation. This will help us uncover the true essence of the sacred liturgy and its essential role in the life of the Church. Only then can we determine what practices best represent the invisible realities of the liturgy and which ones detract from it. It will also allow us to approach *Sacrosanctum Concilium* with an appropriate paradigm while protecting us from falling into the trap of defining certain practices and reforms as "liberal" or "conservative." I cannot overemphasize how important it is to free ourselves of these political categories when thinking about Catholicism in general and the council reforms in particular. We must receive the mystery of our faith and the teachings of the Church with a spirit of humility and a desire for conversion. Only in this way can we ensure that our initiatives are truly from the Lord and not our own wounds or popular opinion.

After our reflection on the essence of the liturgy, we will address certain "hot topics" and claims commonly made about Vatican II's liturgical reforms. Specifically, we will home in on the Holy Mass. Many of us are aware of the tensions currently besetting the Church from both the paracouncil and traditionalists in regard to the sacred liturgy. Some would say it is the most sensitive topic preoccupying the People of God in our time. And so it should be! There is nothing more important in the life of the Church than the sacred liturgy. It will be necessary, therefore, to highlight these places of conflict so as to expose any falsely held notions about Vatican II's instruction on the sacred liturgy. Finally, we will recognize the foundations by which the council promotes legitimate reform and discuss practical ways we can reclaim Vatican II as a powerful ally in restoring the liturgy to its proper place at the center of the life of the Church.

The Origin and Nature of the Liturgy according to Vatican II

Most people think of liturgy as the rites and rituals used for worship. But the rubrics—vital though they may be—do not constitute the essence of the liturgy itself. The sacred liturgy is an all-encompassing reality at the very core of Christian existence. Thus, any genuine conversation about the liturgy cannot be limited to its language, gestures, or norms. It cannot exclusively be a conversation about form; rather, it must first deal with the content of the liturgy, what lies at its root. Clarity about the *content* comes first—only then are we in a position to discern the appropriate *form* that the external practices of the liturgy should take.

Vatican II follows this movement from *content* to *form*. The opening articles of *Sacrosanctum Concilium* do not mention Latin, vernacular, sacred music, church architecture, *ad orientem*, or any other hot-button issues typically associated with the liturgy and Vatican II. Rather, the council starts by outlining a basic history of salvation, inviting the faithful to a deeper understanding of the nature of the liturgy itself as well as its importance in the life of the Church. Articles 5 through 7 are especially important as they embody the overall theology of the liturgy:

> The wonderful works of God among the people of the Old Testament were but a prelude to the work of Christ the Lord in redeeming mankind and giving perfect glory to God. He achieved His task principally by the paschal mystery of His blessed passion, resurrection from the dead, and the glorious ascension. . . . Accordingly, just as Christ was sent by the Father so also he sent the apostles . . . so that they might preach the Gospel . . . To accomplish so great a work, Christ is always present in His Church, especially in her liturgical celebrations . . . Christ, indeed, always associates the Church with Himself in this great work [the sacred liturgy] in which God is perfectly glorified and men are sanctified. (*SSC* 5–7)

The Second Vatican Council describes Christ's mission and the basis of the sacred liturgy in two ways: the *redemption of mankind* and the *perfect glorification of God*. We could summarize these points with the words "reconciliation" and "adoration."

The Sacred Liturgy as Christ's Ministry of Reconciliation

The word "reconciliation" is comprised of three Latin words: *re, con,* and *cilia*. The combination *recon* means "to come back together." *Cilia* is the Latin word for "eyelash." To be reconciled, therefore, means to be eyelash-to-eyelash with God, to be brought into such a profound intimacy that your eyelashes are touching each other. This was the kind of face-to-face intimacy Adam enjoyed with God in the beginning. But we know what happened: Adam sinned, and humanity turned its back on God. To appreciate the full consequences of Adam's sin, we need to understand the creation story and God's original will for humanity.

In the first creation account, we read that God makes man and woman in *imago Dei*, in his own likeness and image. Genesis links Adam and Eve's creation as *imago Dei* with God's declaration that they were "very good" (Gn 1:31). The goodness of humanity is intrinsically linked to its capacity to reflect God's image. The original Hebrew for the phrase "very good" (*tōv meōd*) possesses a moral connotation. To be very good is to be virtuous. In the case of Adam and Eve, the phrase also implies they are without sin. Thus, the way that humanity reveals its essential dignity as *imago Dei* is through a life of virtue and holiness.

This is why Adam's sin against God is so grave. His choice of selfishness over selflessness, his own will as opposed to God's will, was a fundamental contradiction of human nature, a degradation of his very identity. Due to the tempter's deception, Adam and Eve sullied themselves by introducing egoism into the world. Instead of reflecting God's love, they turned inward. In their shame, they attempted to hide from the Creator. What follows is one of the most heartbreaking interactions in all of sacred scripture.

God, looking for his creature, cries out sorrowfully to Adam, "Where are you?" (Gn 3:9). Once again, the original Hebrew is illuminating—a literal translation might read, "From whence do you come?" It is not that God is ignorant of Adam's physical location. It's as if God is asking, "Adam, have you forgotten where you come from? Have you forgotten how much I love you? Where is that beloved son in whom I breathed my own spirit? Why are you scared of me?" A relationship that was once rooted in mutual trust and love has been shattered by anxiety and separation. The man who once walked freely with God "at the breezy time of the day" (Gn 3:8) is now shackled by shame as he huddles in the underbrush like a frightened animal. Because of Adam's sin, humanity's dignity as God's image is now tarnished and our intimacy with God is strained.

Jesus became man to redeem this tragedy. St. Paul was among the first to draw an explicit connection between Adam and Jesus:

> Just as through one person sin entered the world, and through sin, death, and thus death came to all, inasmuch as all sinned. . . . But death reigned from Adam to Moses even over those who did not sin after the pattern of the trespass of Adam, who is the type of the one who was to come. . . . For just as through the disobedience of one person the many were made sinners, so through the obedience of one the many will be made righteous . . . so that, as sin reigned in death, grace also might reign through justification for eternal life through Jesus Christ our Lord. (Rom 5:12, 14, 19–21)

> So, too, it is written, "The first man, Adam, became a living being," the last Adam a life-giving spirit. (1 Cor 15:45)

It is this connection between Adam's failure and Christ's triumph that led St. Paul to call the Lord's mission a "ministry of reconciliation" (2 Cor 5:18). Jesus is the one who comes to restore humanity's original intimacy with the Father; he brings us "eyelash-to-eyelash" with God.

Christ's work of reconciliation against the effects of Adam's sin was a favorite theme of the early Church. St. Melito of Sardis refers to Adam as the "suffering one" and to Jesus as the one "who shares in the suffering one's suffering."[3] St. Ephrem the Syrian speaks of Christ as Adam newly robed in the flesh of the Blessed

Virgin Mary,[4] while St. Gregory of Nyssa calls Christ the remedy of Adam's poison.[5]

But there is more. Since Christ is both fully human and fully divine, he raises our humanity to an entirely new plane of existence. Jesus does not simply restore the original goodness of humanity. He also imbues our human nature with his own divine life, raising us to a dignity previously unimaginable. St. Symeon the New Theologian summarizes it well:

> God the Word, Who by nature has no flesh, took from us and became man, which He was not before. He imparts His own divinity to those who believe in Him—something which neither angels nor men had ever had before—and, by adoption and by grace, they become gods who before were not.[6]

The process St. Symeon describes is called *divinization*. That's not a term you're likely to hear in the average parish homily. Nonetheless, it is essential to understanding salvation. Put simply, divinization—also called deification—is humanity's sharing in the very life of God by merit of Christ's own humanity. The second person of the Blessed Trinity became man, like us in all things but sin (Heb 4:15). As such, he represents all of humanity to the Father as "the firstborn of all creation" (Col 1:15). Jesus replaces Adam as the new reference point of humanity. In place of Adam's faithlessness, disobedience, and self-centeredness, Jesus' fidelity, devotion, sacrifice, and love form the foundations of a new creation. Christ's life expands the horizons of our humanity. In him, our human nature becomes "supernatural," literally "built up" or "augmented."

This is accomplished through the Passion, Death, Resurrection, and Ascension of Jesus Christ. In his Passion and Death, the disobedience of Adam is rectified and the penalty of his disobedience—death—is paid. Through the Resurrection, death is conquered and transformed from a tragic ending into a doorway to eternal life. Finally, in Christ's Ascension, humanity is afforded an active participation in the intimacy of the Blessed Trinity. Right now, at this very moment, there is a human being with a human body sharing in the life of God. His body opens up the heart of God for us so that we too might rejoice in its glory and receive its grace. The profundity of this mystery is captured beautifully in an ancient hymn of the Eastern Catholic Church: "O Jesus . . . you ascended into heaven and you seated *me* at the right hand of the Father. In amazement before all these miracles I sing to you."[7]

Through his sacrifice and Resurrection, Jesus reconciles humanity with God, taking us with himself to dwell in the heart of divine love. With this in mind, St. Paul asserts that "whoever is in Christ is a new creation: the old things have passed away; behold, new things have come. And all this is from God, who has reconciled us to himself through Christ and given us the ministry of reconciliation" (2 Cor 5:17–18).

Returning to our original point, when we say the word "liturgy," we are referring to Christ's ministry of reconciliation by which he continues to actively maintain the communion of creation with its Creator through his Paschal Mystery. The reconciliation accomplished by Christ is not a mere act of the past; it continues to be effective through the sacred liturgy. Every time we baptize a child, anoint the sick, hear a Confession, or celebrate Holy Mass, Jesus is reconciling the world to the Father. Thus the Church says in Eucharistic Prayer III:

> Look, we pray, upon the oblation of your Church and, recognizing the sacrificial Victim by whose death you willed to reconcile us to yourself, grant that we, who are nourished by the Body and Blood of your Son and filled with his Holy Spirit, may become one body, one spirit in Christ. . . . May this Sacrifice of our reconciliation, we pray, O Lord, advance the peace and salvation of all the world.[8]

The Sacred Liturgy as Christ's Adoration of the Father

Keeping in mind these considerations on the nature of the human person as *imago Dei* and Jesus' ministry of reconciliation continued through the sacred liturgy, we can now reflect on another important verse regarding Adam from the Book of Genesis: God places Adam in the garden to "cultivate and care for it" (Gn 2:15). *The primary responsibility of Adam is to cultivate the garden.* At first glance, this seems like a passing detail. But a look at the original language shows us something quite profound. The word "cultivate" in Genesis 2:15 translates the Hebrew word *'abedah*, from the root word *'ābad*. It is an incredibly important word in Judaism, employed more than 280 times in the Old Testament. In the Books of Numbers and Joshua, it is a term reserved for priests, signifying their ministry of worship to God (see Nm 3:7–8, where it is sometimes translated "maintaining," and Jos 22:27, which uses *'ābad* to describe the priests' duty to perform or "provide for" the rituals of various offerings and sacrifices). Most famously, it is the word God uses when giving Moses the Ten Commandments: "You shall not bow down before [other gods] or serve (*tā'ābeḏêm*, from *'ābad*) them" (Ex 20:5). The use of this verb by the Jewish authors of Genesis clearly indicates that they saw Adam as a liturgical figure. Adam, as a being composed of both body and soul, was an instantiation of the world of spirit and the world of the flesh. He is seen as the mediator of a covenant between God and creation. This is a direct consequence of his being created in the image of God.

Thus, ancient Jewish and Christian scholars identify Adam as a priest. Before anything else, Adam is called to represent all of creation by glorifying God. The fourth-century bishop Severian of Gabala reminds us that Adam could achieve this task by following God's command not to touch the tree of life and death.[9] Obedience was the foundation for Adam's priestly ministry. He was to live a life of holiness and loving devotion to his Creator—in other words, orthodoxy, or "right worship" of God. When Adam chose self-glorification over the glory of God, he failed in this sacred responsibility and introduced disharmony into creation. Where there was once cooperation, there is now enmity: "To the man he said: Because you listened to your wife and ate from the tree about which I commanded you, You shall not eat from it, Cursed is the ground because of you! In toil you shall eat its yield all the days of your life" (Gn 3:17).

Jesus becomes man, therefore, not only to divinize humanity but also, as the new high priest, to restore right worship of the Father. Put simply, Jesus comes to adore the Father. The word "adoration" comes from the Latin *ad-ora*, literally "mouth-to-mouth." Adoration presupposes reconciliation and is its natural consequence. One must be eyelash-to-eyelash in order to be mouth-to-mouth. Through reconciliation with God, we get close enough to kiss him. In Jesus, humanity is reoriented toward God, no longer navel-gazing but looking toward the Father. Even more, humanity is afforded the opportunity of sharing in the same intimacy and communion with the Father that Jesus himself enjoys.

Nowhere is this made more evident than in those beautiful words prayed by Christ to his Father the night before his Passion: "Everything of mine is yours and everything of yours is mine, and I have been glorified in them [the apostles]. And now I will no longer be in the world, but they are in the world, while I am coming to you. Holy Father, keep them in your name that you have given me, so that they may be one just as we are" (Jn 17:10–11). The Church traditionally calls this section of John 17 the High Priestly Prayer of Jesus. In these words, the Lord is crystal clear in his intention to establish the Church and intercede on her behalf for all time as the priest of the new covenant. Likewise, it is a summary and exposition of his ministry and mission. He does not come to adore the Father in isolation, but with his people. He desires to open up his intimacy with the Father so that all those who are in his name might relish their mystical love.

It was no coincidence that the Lord celebrated the Last Supper before saying the High Priestly Prayer. The Eucharist is the principal manifestation of Christ's priesthood. Furthermore, in the Last Supper, Jesus provides the way by which we share in his adoration of and intimacy with the Father. The Passion he is about to endure is not intended to be a memory, but a living reality constantly present in the heart of the Church. Thus, "on the night when He was betrayed, our Savior instituted the Eucharistic sacrifice of His Body and Blood. He did this in order to perpetuate the sacrifice of the Cross throughout the centuries" (*SSC* 47). It is a sacrifice established "once for all" as an act of perpetual adoration to the Father (Heb 10:10).

There is a crucial point here: the Eucharist is not primarily Jesus' gift to us. It is first and foremost his gift to the Father.[10] We are not the center of attention in the liturgy. It is not about us. Rather, it is Jesus actively incorporating our lives into *his* worship of the Father. We are not the origin of the liturgy; we are participants in it. This is a point that was skewed by the paracouncil in the years following Vatican II. In an attempt to emphasize the role of the congregation, some people unduly accentuated the communal aspect of the liturgy while suppressing its most vital component: sacrifice. The Mass became primarily an act of the worshipping community as opposed to an act rooted in the activity of Christ.

The consequences of such a mentality are severe. If the liturgy becomes *our* thing, then it is subject to our will, not the will of God. Slowly but surely, we lose focus on what really matters. Our priority becomes the music, the preaching, the entertainment, the technology. We start trusting in our own devices to ensure right worship—all the while neglecting the One who is the perfect offering.

This is unsustainable. People do not come to church for our ideas. They come to encounter God. If we attempt to be competitive with the church down the street by getting hipper music or installing projection screens, we are already losing sight of our most treasured asset. There will always be some other church that has more money, better resources, and newer technology. But, thankfully, that is not what makes our experience of worship valuable. Good liturgy is not a thing of this world; it is the work of Christ, and it is precious in the Father's sight. All we have to do is trust: Trust that the liturgy is enough. Trust that the prayers, rituals, and rubrics will suffice if we practice them obediently and reverently.

Active Participation: The Basic Principle of Reform

Everything we just learned provides the backdrop for Vatican II's understanding of the sacred liturgy. Informed by the scriptures and writings of the Church Fathers, the council sought to renew a sense of the sacred in the hearts of the faithful. Its goal was to foster a full appreciation of the liturgy in the hearts of God's people. Fostering active participation in the liturgy was clearly a top priority of the council's liturgical reform.

Yet, the notion of active participation remains one of the most misrepresented of Vatican II's teachings. Unfortunately, in the years immediately following the council, the phrase was "very quickly misunderstood to mean something external, entailing a need for general activity, as if as many people as possible, as often as possible, should be visibly engaged in action."[11] This fallout didn't just appear out of thin air—it was preceded by several centuries of philosophical developments—but it all boils down to a superficial definition of what it means to be active, as well as a failure to recognize the principal action of the liturgy itself.

What Do We Mean by "Active"?

In our utilitarian society, to be active is usually taken to mean something like, "*I* have to *do* something." As a result of this mentality, the council's notion of active participation was all too easily reduced to a mere *activism*. Both clergy and laity felt the need to overemphasize the role of the faith community, ensuring that everyone had a part to play. Music needed to be upbeat and fun, the preaching needed to be interactive and stimulating, there needed to be lay ministers fulfilling liturgical roles, the lighting and screens needed to be state-of-the-art. Most important of all, the liturgy could not appear boring.

In the wake of Vatican II, some priests feel pressured or obligated to enhance certain parts of the Mass, even though the council expressly forbids any priest from adding, removing, or changing anything in the liturgy on his own authority (*SSC* 22). There is a temptation to think the liturgy is insufficient on its own or lacks the ability to inspire God's people in and of itself. *Maybe it needs a helping hand.*

But this is deeply misguided. Tinkering with the liturgy to make it more engaging or entertaining indirectly forms communities to believe that *their* actions and feelings are the basis of liturgical action. The liturgy develops an egocentric character, with the needs and wants of the community overshadowing the essential nature of the mystery.

Many parish priests I've spoken with have encountered evidence of this very mentality. How often we hear people say they are going to a Protestant service down the street because they have better music or the preaching is more enthusiastic. "I just get more out of their services than from going to Mass." This kind of thinking is the direct result of God's people not being properly educated on the purpose of worship as well as pastors unduly prioritizing external action instead of forming the people's hearts in the true spirit of the liturgy.

Suffice it to say, this was not Vatican II's intention when the council penned the phrase "active participation"! Whereas before Vatican II, there was sometimes a lack of adequate participation due to a defect in understanding the role of the laity, now we find ourselves on the other side of the spectrum. Today, there is more activity during the liturgy but not necessarily a genuine participation of the faithful. Owing to an excess of external action, there tends to be less appreciation for interior action and the responsibility of the laity to relive in themselves the sentiments and thoughts of Christ.[12]

So what is Vatican II's vision for active participation? To answer this question, we first need to rehabilitate the Catholic definition of "action" and its relation to the liturgy.

Actio is one of the rare Latin words that ends with a masculine vowel, "o," yet possesses a feminine connotation. In the Greco-Roman mind, therefore, action is associated with feminine characteristics. This is no doubt due to the ancients' wonder at the phenomenon of fertility. The woman receives, yet in her receptivity she does the greatest activity of all: the generation of human life. Long stretches of pregnancy are outwardly uneventful—but all the while, a miracle is being formed. The woman is not consciously willing the child or working in an obvious way to knit it in her womb. Rather, in her meekness, the marvel unfolds within her. Daily, she contemplates its grandeur and abides in its mystery as she feels the child grow. At the moment of birth, her receptivity and contemplation give way to amazement at the fruit of her womb.

All of this is to say that *action is primarily receptive.* Reception precedes action; action presupposes reception. To be active does not mean "to do stuff." It primarily means to be still and receive. It is a conscious recognition of *what is happening to you,* not *what you are doing.* This is a fundamental principle of the spiritual life. We do not grow in holiness by our volition alone, but by receiving Christ's grace. "It was not you who chose me, but I who chose you and appointed you to go and bear fruit that will remain" (Jn 15:16). And again, "We love because he first loved us" (1 Jn 4:19).

Nowhere is this better exemplified than in the life of the Blessed Virgin Mary. Gabriel appeared to her proclaiming, "Behold, you will conceive in your womb and bear a son" (Lk 1:31). Mary responded, "May it be done to me according to your word" (Lk 1:38). God took this receptive spirit and made it the most fruitful activity in world history as Mary conceived the second person of the Trinity. She contemplated these events in her heart and responded to the mission of the Son by staying at his side until the very end, at the foot of the Cross. Thus, the Blessed Mother teaches us the real basis of active participation: to consciously recognize God's presence and peacefully allow his will to inform our actions.

No wonder Christians profess Mary as Mother and Model of the Church! In her we find the disposition of soul necessary for active participation in the sacred liturgy. No one more perfectly embodies the spirit of the liturgy than the Virgin Mary. For this reason, all generations call her blessed, and within her heart is revealed the thoughts, longings, and aspirations of the world (see Luke 1:48, 2:35).

God is the main actor of the sacred liturgy and its central focus. It is he who initiates the action, not us. Active participation does not only mean singing hymns, serving as an extraordinary minister of the Eucharist, or ushering people during Communion. These are all good things, and there is a place for them in certain circumstances. But they are secondary, not primary, to active participation. Before all else, active participation means to be contemplatively and prayerfully engaged in the liturgical action of the Mass—the traditions and official prayers of the Church. Thus, the "real 'action' of the liturgy in which we are all supposed to participate is the action of God Himself. This is what is new and distinctive about Christian liturgy: God Himself acts and does what is essential."[13] Any time the sacred books or rites mention "action" in the liturgy, it is primarily referring to the Eucharistic Prayer offered by the priest and actively contemplated by the faithful.[14]

All supplementary liturgical ministries—choir, Eucharistic ministers, readers, sacristans, greeters, and so on—must be guided by this fundamental understanding of active participation. Doing so will surely change the attitude with which each person enacts his or her respective ministry. Choir directors will be keener to select appropriate hymnody that fosters solemnity and contemplation instead of entertainment. Readers and Eucharistic ministers will arrive earlier to Mass so that they can sit in prayerful meditation, preparing their hearts to serve. Priests will maintain a spirit of prayerful vigil in the sacristy as they vest for the Sacrifice of the Mass. The main assembly will remain a space of sacred silence both before and after liturgies, allowing the People of God to meditate on the Lord's saving mysteries. Recovering the true meaning of the council's intention for "active participation" can bring a profound change of culture to our parishes.

Rediscovering Sacred Silence

To this end, sacred silence before, during, and after liturgies is essential. The *General Instruction of the Roman Missal* (GIRM) is a set of regulations on the Mass intended to educate and govern the priest and the laity on how to celebrate the sacred liturgy. In regard to our current topic, the GIRM is clear in its insistence on the role of sacred silence in fostering active participation:

> Sacred silence also, as part of the celebration, is to be observed at the designated times. Its nature, however, depends on the moment when it occurs in the different parts of the celebration. For in the Penitential Act and again after the invitation to pray, individuals recollect themselves; whereas after a reading or after the Homily, all meditate briefly on what they have heard; then after Communion, they praise God in their hearts and pray to him. Even before the celebration itself, it is a praise-worthy practice for silence to be observed in the church, in the sacristy, in the vesting room, and in adjacent areas, so that all may dispose themselves to carry out the sacred celebration in a devout and fitting manner.[15]

Too often, Eucharistic celebrations are filled with noise. People are never afforded a moment to rest in the Lord. As soon as we are invited to repent of our sins, we start reciting the Confiteor without having a moment to recollect God's mercy. After the homily, people applaud before the priest jumps straight into the Creed. Communion is immediately followed by a choir piece and parish announcements. Silence is treated like a stopgap or a transition between different activities instead of an integral part of the liturgy. Yet, we know that God speaks most clearly in the realm of silence. The Lord's voice is not rambunctious. It is still and small (see 1 Kings 19:11–13). Silence is a prerequisite of active participation.

The simple reintegration of intentional moments of silence into the liturgy will prove vital in reclaiming the Second Vatican Council's vision of the liturgy, which clearly states the role of silence in promoting active participation (*SSC* 30). I have seen the effects of silence personally in my own parish ministry. During the Penitential Act, as I ask the people to join me in recollecting our sins, I typically take a long pause for sacred silence. The same is done between readings, after the homily, and after Holy Communion. I cannot overstate how this practice can deepen the spiritual awareness of a parish community. Even children's behavior changes at school Masses. Silence reminds all of us of the reason we are in this building and the importance of what we are doing. In a world overrun with constant stimulation, silence is a powerful tool.

We must avoid burdening the liturgy with unnecessary noise; without intentional silence, we risk becoming a "resounding gong or a clashing cymbal" (1 Cor 13:1). There is also no need to rush the liturgy. The goal of Mass is not to get people in and out in an hour. The goal is to help them encounter the living God and make them saints. It is impossible to do so without prayerful silence.

All that being said, it would be imprudent to begin practicing sacred silence without first catechizing the people. This is true when introducing anything new to a faith community. In our attempt to reclaim Vatican II's original intention of solemnity and sacred-ness in the liturgy, we must be patient. Many parishes have gone through decades of paraconciliar liturgies. There are "traditions" and local customs that develop and to which people become quite attached. For example, I was once assigned to a parish where it was customary to applaud for the priest after his homily. The first time it happened to me, I was shell-shocked. And although my homily was serviceable, it definitely did not merit applause! When I spoke to the pastor about it, he said the people had been doing that for years. Eventually, we decided to address the topic with the parish-ioners. I spoke at all the Masses, giving a reflection on the proper way to honor God in the liturgy and the purpose of maintaining silence after the homily so as to reflect on the message and allow Christ to convert our hearts. The talk was short, sweet, and to the point. I was lighthearted and uncritical.

When I next preached at Mass, a few forgetful listeners started clapping, but it quickly died off. We then spent about two minutes sitting in silence before starting the Creed. The whole character of the Mass was different. The people were more engaged in the Eucharistic Prayer and responded to their various parts with enthu-siasm. After Mass, droves of people came up and thanked me. One of them gleefully told me, "Thank God you said something. We have been doing that for years and I honestly don't even know why. Most of the homilies don't deserve applause anyways." I decided to take it as a compliment.

"But wait," I can hear you asking, "won't all this silence make the liturgy too somber or boring?" I've found the complete oppo-site to be true! Appropriate moments of silence ensure that the congregation is actively aware of what is taking place. It is also a clear indicator that what we are doing in this space is special and not just another form of entertainment.

The notion of active participation was a central theme in Vat-ican II's reforms of the liturgy. More than anything, the council fathers hoped to rekindle a flame in the hearts of God's people for the sacred liturgy. The council envisioned a community of people at prayer and in watchful vigil of the Eucharistic mystery. If we are to reclaim Vatican II's hope for active participation, we must re-evaluate the culture of our local parishes and catechize ourselves to be a community of contemplation. Likewise, we must provide an environment that fosters prayer in our sacred spaces and throughout the liturgy itself.

Ad Orientem or *Versus Populum*?

Now it is time to get into a couple of hot-button topics. Our reflections up to this point show us that the liturgy is not just the rites and traditions associated with the Mass, but rather encompasses the entire act of salvation and its continued manifestation through the sacramental life of the Church. Likewise, we understand that Vatican II hoped to inspire a more active participation of the faithful not so much through external action, but rather through a prayerful and catechized appreciation of the liturgy. Thus, when it comes to discerning practical aspects of liturgical rituals, we have to ask what gestures, words, and actions best transmit the mystery. Even though there may be multiple opinions on the matter, tradition maintains several long-standing practices that speak to the essence of the Catholic liturgy. One of these practices is *ad orientem*, or "facing the east."

Put briefly, in a Mass celebrated *ad orientem*, the priest faces east during certain points of the Mass and faces the people at others, depending on his role at that moment in the liturgy. When he is speaking directly to God, he joins the people in facing toward the east as an intercessor on their behalf. The priest faces the people when he is speaking in the person of Christ to the congregation. A Mass that is celebrated *versus populum*, on the other hand, does not make use of the *ad orientem* posture at any point in the liturgy, even when the priest is not speaking directly to the people.

Rather, the priest faces the people for the entire Mass regardless of his role at any point in the liturgy. (It is important to note that a Mass celebrated ad orientem can still use the vernacular language, and ad orientem is not a synonym for "the extraordinary form of the Mass.")

Unfortunately, this topic is unnecessarily politicized and tense. Some people see *ad orientem* as a relic of the past and a hallmark of traditionalist Catholicism. They do not understand why the priest would "turn his back on the people," and they interpret this posture as unpastoral, clericalist, and inconsiderate of the laity's participation in the liturgy. Thankfully, Vatican II got rid of this old idea, right? Not so fast!

Ad orientem is not mentioned a single time in the Second Vatican Council's Constitution on the Sacred Liturgy. The council did not forbid it, nor did any post-conciliar documents suppress it. The claim that Vatican II got rid of *ad orientem* is simply not true. Likewise, *versus populum*, or "facing the people," is not mentioned in the council's document on the liturgy. There is a passing comment in a post-conciliar document that "the main altar should preferably be freestanding, to permit walking around it and celebration facing the people."[16] But this in no way forbids or excludes the use of *ad orientem*. In fact, the current Roman Missal presumes the priest is facing east during the Eucharistic Prayer and Communion Rite as can be seen in rubric 127 of the Order of Mass, which instructs the priest to turn toward the people when offering the Sign of Peace.

On the surface, this may seem like an insignificant discussion. Why does it matter what direction the priest faces when celebrating Mass? But there are serious philosophical and spiritual consequences at stake in this conversation. As beings composed of body and soul, what we do with our bodies and how we do it matters. Our gestures, words, and environment affect our disposition. The way we celebrate the liturgy, down to its smallest detail, sends a message and forms people's hearts for or against the truth of salvation.

That being said, let us dive deeper into the origins of *ad orientem* and why Vatican II, in perfect continuity with the history of the Church, did not suppress it.

Traditionally, east is the proper direction of liturgical prayer for Jews and Christians. The sacredness of the east began with a longing to return to the Garden of Eden as St. Basil the Great teaches us in his work *On the Holy Spirit*: "For this reason we all look to the east in our prayers, although few know that this is because we are seek-·ing the ancient fatherland, which God planted in Eden."[17] After the fall, Eden—which "lies in the east" (Gn 2:8)—became a focal point of worship for the Jewish people, a symbol of humanity's desire to regain intimacy with God and restore communion with creation. This reverence for the east was exponentially heightened after the construction of the Temple in Jerusalem—the east was where God was revealing himself to humanity and maintaining his covenant with Israel. Thus, all Jews pray toward the Temple as a means of unity with the sacrificial cult of Jerusalem and a sign of hope in the promise of a coming Messiah. The most inspiring and mystical example of the east's significance in Judaism comes from Ezekiel's vision of the restoration of Israel in which he sees God's glory "coming from the east," where the new temple "facing the east" flows with life-giving water cascading eastward (see Ez 40–47).

In Christ, Ezekiel's vision is realized. Jesus is the new Temple, rising from the east. The temple of his body is torn open with a lance as life-giving waters flow from his pierced heart. The ancient Church was quick to recognize the meaning of Jesus' Paschal Mystery and its relation to these prophecies about the east as can be seen in the original liturgy of Christian initiation. Catechumens preparing for Baptism were required to face west when making the baptismal promises to renounce Satan and his works. Then, they turned east to affirm their faith in Jesus Christ and the Church. It was understood that Jesus is the fulfillment of the promises associated with the east. It is he who reclaims the dignity Adam lost in the garden, restores humanity's communion with the created world, and establishes an everlasting cult of worship transcending the temporary sacrifices of the Temple. Furthermore, Jesus promises that he will come again to bring all things into one. Thus, eastward-facing liturgical prayer was a gesture of expectation as the Church awaited the second coming of her Bridegroom. St. Germanus of Constantinople synthesizes this early Christian theology in his writings *On the Divine Liturgy*:

> Praying toward the east is handed down by the holy apostles, as is everything else. This is because the comprehensible sun of righteousness, Christ our God, appeared on earth in those regions of the east where the perceptible sun rises, as the prophet says: 'Orient is his name' (Zech. 6:12); and 'Bow before the Lord all the earth, who ascended to the heaven of heavens in the east' (Ps. 67:34); and 'Let us prostrate ourselves in the place where his feet have stood' (Ps. 67:34); and again, 'The feet of the Lord shall stand upon the Mount of Olives in the east' (Zech. 14:4). The prophets also speak thus because of our fervent hope of receiving again the paradise in Eden, as well as the dawn of the brightness of the second coming of Christ our God, from the east.[18]

Facing east, therefore, has a fourfold significance in Catholicism. First, it testifies to the continuity of salvation history, for the Church is the people in whom God fulfills all the promises of Israel. Second, it shows our orientation toward Christ, the God who enters into history and reveals himself concretely in a specific place and time. Third, it is a sign of our unity with creation in adoring Christ, the new Adam. As the sun rises in the east, so do the hands of the priest lifting up the host. When the priest and congregation join one another facing east, they cooperate with creation in adoring Jesus in a single act of praise. Finally, it shows that we are a pilgrim people expectantly awaiting the Second Coming of the

Lord. We are not here to dwell in one another's company or gaze at each other. We are not a self-enclosed community. Rather, we are a people on the way, a Church that joyfully sings "Come, Lord Jesus!" as we face toward the risen Lord (Rv 22:20).

All these points—rooted in the theology and tradition of the Church—affirm the spiritual significance of *ad orientem*. So, if *versus populum* is not mentioned or encouraged by Vatican II, why did it become the standard? Then-cardinal Ratzinger identifies two main reasons. First, some liturgists after the council referenced several churches in Rome—most notably St. Peter's Basilica—that have freestanding altars and see the priest celebrating Mass facing the people. However, as Ratzinger reminds us, this is a misreading of the architectural layout. Due to topographical challenges, St. Peter's was built facing west. "Thus, if the celebrating priest wanted—as the Christian tradition of prayer demands—to face east, he had to stand behind the [altar] and look . . . toward the people."[19] Another popular claim was that facing the people more closely resembled the Last Supper and emphasized the communal-meal character of the Eucharist. However, "nowhere in Christian antiquity could have arisen the idea of having to 'face the people' to preside at a meal [that is, the Last Supper]. The communal character of a meal was emphasized by just the opposite disposition: the fact that all participants were on the same side of the table."[20] Yet these arguments "seemed in the end so persuasive that after the council (which says nothing about 'turning towards the people') new altars were set up everywhere, and today celebration *versus populum* really does look like a characteristic fruit of Vatican II's liturgical renewal."[21]

Let me be clear: I am not saying we should start celebrating Mass *ad orientem* tomorrow. Nor is celebrating the Mass *versus populum* invalid or illicit. The point I am making is that there is no basis to the claim that *ad orientem* is against the spirit of Vatican II. Vatican II does not discourage the use of *ad orientem*. Furthermore, as Cardinal Ratzinger reminds us, facing the people for the entirety of the Mass is a paraconciliar novelty that disrupts the structure and focus of the sacred liturgy. It unnecessarily clericalizes the Eucharist by making the priest the center of attention while simultaneously enclosing the faith community into itself. Thus, we begin to think that

> everything depends on him [the priest]. We have to see him, to respond to him, to be involved in what he is doing. His creativity sustains the whole thing . . . less and less is God in the picture. More and more important is what is done by the human beings who meet here and do not like to subject themselves to a "pre-determined pattern." The turning of the priest toward the people has turned the community into a self-enclosed circle.[22]

An experience I had as a newly ordained priest solidified Ratzinger's point in my own heart. After my ordination to the priesthood, I took a thanksgiving pilgrimage with my family to the Holy Land. During that pilgrimage, I was able to celebrate Mass in the cave of St. Jerome at Bethlehem. Due to the antiquity of the chapel, the altar was constructed *ad orientem*. I have to be honest that it felt a bit awkward in the beginning. I was trained to say Mass *versus populum*. But all that changed the moment of the elevation. Typically, when I raise the chalice at Mass, I only see my own reflection in the metal; the priest is alone and at the center. But when I elevated the chalice after the words of institution, I did not see my own reflection, but the faces of God's people. Every soul who was entrusting their prayers to me as a priest was present in that chalice with the Blood of Christ. Furthermore, when I looked up, I did not see empty space or a drop ceiling, but the crucifix. In a single view, I saw the summary of my priestly vocation as I gazed simultaneously at both my people and my Lord. At that moment, I knew it was right. It made sense. I, as the priest, was uniting myself with the People of God, raising them in adoration through Christ to the heavenly Father. That action was not just my own nor was I making it in isolation. The hopes and dreams of the whole Church resided in that chalice. I know that my experience in Bethlehem is not a special case. Many of my brother priests have shared similar experiences after celebrating Mass *ad orientem* the first time.

As I mentioned before, when it comes to discerning forms of celebrating the liturgy, we must set aside our personal preferences and ask objectively: What practices most perfectly reflect the reality of what is taking place during the Mass? What words and gestures best convey the essence of the liturgy and act in continuity with the history of Catholicism? It is these guiding questions that prompted the council fathers to repeatedly assert their commitment to enact all reform in obedience to the "sound tradition" of the Church (*SSC* 4, 23). *Ad orientem* does not represent a threat to the People of God's participation in the liturgy, nor is it a rejection of the pastoral dimension of the Eucharist. On the contrary, *ad orientem* is a tried-and-true practice of the Church that beautifully captures the original intention of the liturgy, which addresses both God and the congregation, not exclusively one or the other.

As we seek to reclaim Vatican II and the theology of *Sacrosanctum Concilium*, the reintegration of *ad orientem* into the common liturgical experience of the faithful will prove indispensable. That being said, it must be done in a spirit of pastoral charity, patience, and prudence. As with all progression in the Church, adequate catechesis is necessary first. After several decades of *versus populum* liturgies, it will take time to form people's minds and hearts. For years, *ad orientem* has been regarded as an unpastoral gesture in which the priest "turns his back" on the people. What the wisdom of the ancient Church teaches us, however, is that *ad orientem* is not the priest neglecting the congregation, but the priest *joining them* in a single act of praise as he represents their needs and aspirations to God in the person of Christ. It is an act of *inclusion*, not exclusion.

On a practical note, there are several steps we can take to begin appreciating the significance of *ad orientem* as a foundational form of the liturgy. First, we need to reexamine our understanding of the Eucharist as a sacrificial action. In the 1960s and 1970s, it was popular to describe the Eucharist as a celebration meal or fraternal banquet. Although these titles are not wrong, they are secondary. Before all else, the Mass is a sacrifice, as is stated multiple times by the council. It is the action of Christ crucified giving himself to the Father on our behalf. Thus, in those moments when Jesus is manifesting his sacrifice through the priest—that is, the Eucharistic Prayer—the priest joins the people in facing toward the east as a sign of unity with creation in adoring the mysteries and prophecies of Christ (*ad orientem*). The Mass is a celebration *because* it is a sacrifice. Our sharing at the table of the Lord *flows from* our witnessing the sacrifice at the altar of the Cross. That is why the high point of the Mass is not the reception of Holy Communion (also known as "the meal"), but the doxology: "Through him, with him, and in him. . . ." It is with these words, while the priest raises the body, blood, soul, and divinity of Jesus, that salvation is made present in our midst.

Second, we need pastoral catechesis. This is what Vatican II wittingly refers to as the "liturgical apostolate" (*SSC* 45). Having talks or missions on the Holy Mass in which the speaker also discusses the history and theology of *ad orientem* is very beneficial. I have found that when people learn the reason for something, they are a lot more likely to embrace it.

When I first spoke about *ad orientem* at a retreat, I was amazed at the parishioners' response. We had a day of recollection for our extraordinary ministers of Holy Communion at which I reflected on the sacredness of the Mass. When I arrived at the section on the Eucharistic Prayer, I mentioned *ad orientem*. I presented it matter-of-factly and with no ulterior motive. The main point was simply to highlight the spiritual significance of the posture. I spoke about it for maybe five minutes and then proceeded with the rest of the reflection. After the talk, several Eucharistic ministers came up to me awestruck. "Father, why don't we celebrate Mass *ad orientem* anymore?" Even some of the elderly who grew up celebrating the extraordinary form of the Mass mentioned that they had never heard *ad orientem* explained that way. I did not receive a single negative response from the laity. They were inspired and touched by the tradition.

Once a significant amount of catechesis is provided and the people warm up to the idea of *ad orientem*, priests can discern ways to gradually normalize the practice. There are all sorts of creative ways to implement it. One approach is to make it something special by tying it to a high liturgical feast such as Holy Thursday or Corpus Christi. Another option would be to ask the parishioners what they think and what days they would like to celebrate Mass *ad orientem*.

Yet another approach could be the modified version of *ad orientem* suggested by Cardinal Ratzinger.[23] This is especially helpful in faith communities that may not be open to or ready for *ad orientem*. Ratzinger suggests placing a crucifix and candles on the altar to create a sort of screen. The intention is to have a physical reminder for the faithful that the Eucharistic Prayer is not oriented toward the people, but focused on God. The most important thing is to be patient and persevere. Change does not come easily or suddenly. It may take years to implement Vatican II's vision for the liturgy—and that is okay. We priests must remain faithful, charitable, and pastoral. The People of God are open and willing to be formed.

Whatever your preference and perspective on *ad orientem* and *versus populum*, the important point here is that Vatican II did not suppress or dissuade *ad orientem*. If the beauty and rich tradition of *ad orientem* resonate with you, that is no obstacle to being a Vatican II Catholic! Indeed, I would argue that a preference for *ad orientem* aligns in an especially deep way with the true spirit and logic of Vatican II's liturgical reforms.

Latin and the Vernacular

Let us just say it up front: *Vatican II did not get rid of Latin.* In reality, the complete opposite is true. The council not only supports the retention of Latin in the sacred liturgy but asserts it is necessary to the preservation of Catholic tradition. Paragraph 54 of *Sacrosanctum Concilium* is especially clear when it says that the vernacular "may be" used at certain times, whereas Latin "must be" used; further, pastors of souls are responsible for ensuring that "the faithful are able to say or sing together in Latin those parts of the ordinary of the Mass which pertain to them" (*SSC* 54). To put it simply, Vatican II affirms that teaching God's people the Latin prayers of the Mass is not an option, but a pastoral obligation! Although there are people who see Latin and the vernacular as mutually exclusive, the Second Vatican Council offers a different insight. Latin and the vernacular are not antithetical but rather are intended to be essentially cooperative in the liturgy, informing one another and building one another up.

With this in mind, St. Paul VI published a wonderful little book of Latin prayers and chants in 1974. The booklet is entitled *Jubilate Deo*. It was distributed by the Holy See to every bishop and religious superior in the world, who were asked to use the booklet so as

> to make it easier for Christians to achieve unity and spiritual harmony with their brothers and with the living traditions of the past. Hence it is that those who are trying to improve the quality of congregational singing cannot refuse to give Gregorian chant the place which is due to it. . . . In presenting the Holy Father's gift to you, may I at the same time remind you of the desire which he has often expressed that the Conciliar constitution on the liturgy be increasingly better implemented.[24]

St. Paul VI's promotion of this text indicates the true intention of Vatican II and its vision to retain the priority of Latin in the liturgy.

Sadly, like many other things supported by Vatican II, this booklet was barely utilized after the council. As a result, the vast majority of Catholics nowadays cannot join their brothers and sisters around the world in worshiping God with a single tongue. We must not underestimate the damage this failure has done to the People of God. In fact, it has led to an identity crisis in the Church as parish communities become more isolated by local customs, hymns, and liturgical expressions than united by the age-old patrimony of our predecessors.

As a Hispanic, my mother was adamant that I learn Spanish. This allowed me to communicate with my Puerto Rican grand-father and grandmother as well as appreciate the heritage of my family's culture. I often hear descendants of immigrants express regret that their parents never taught them Italian, German, or Gaelic. Likewise, I hear many young Catholics express regret that their pastors and lay leaders never taught them the language of their Mother, the Church. Language is not an accidental or insig-nificant thing. How we speak is the result of thousands of years and millions of lives. To say the Creed in the same language as St. Francis of Assisi or St. Teresa of Ávila means something. It is a sign of the Church's harmony throughout the ages and a testament of our communion with the saints.

As a millennial Catholic, I was not raised with Latin in the liturgy. Thankfully, due to the inspiration of Pope Benedict XVI, I decided to study it in seminary and worked diligently for hours in the library to accustom myself to the parts of the Mass. Yet, even then it was rarely used in our seminary, so I could not appreciate the fundamental role of Latin in the context of the sacred liturgy. It was only when I attended World Youth Day in Madrid that I saw the genius of Vatican II's teaching.

The closing Mass was celebrated in multiple languages: Spanish, Italian, French, Portuguese, and more. For most of the liturgy, the young adults were disengaged as only a small percentage could speak certain languages. Yet, when it came time for the Our Father, Pope Benedict began to chant in Latin. For the first time that Mass, I heard thousands of voices sing in unison. I only made it through two lines of the Pater Noster before I started crying. It was one of the most inspiring experiences of my life. I looked out on the sea of youth, flags waving proudly from every continent of this good earth, singing with one voice. "This is the Church," I thought to myself. "This is Pentecost."

Latin is one of the more politicized topics of our time. We can no longer afford such an attitude. To reject, suppress, or disavow the Latin language is to directly contradict the Second Vatican Council. It is not a question of being traditional or liberal. When we shelter the faithful from their Mother's native tongue, we do them a disservice and refuse an avenue of deep holiness for their lives.

Furthermore, we can no longer allow the disuse of the Latin language within the liturgy to be a bludgeon in the hands of traditionalists seeking to discredit the Second Vatican Council. The teaching of Vatican II is clear: Latin was never and should never be suppressed in the sacred liturgy. It is to be revered with pride of place in divine worship and actively taught to God's people. This teaching of the council was reiterated by the two premier interpreters of Vatican II, St. John Paul II and Pope Benedict XVI. St. John Paul II often highlighted the importance of maintaining the use of Latin, as is exemplified in his apostolic letter *Vicesimus Quintus Annus*.[25] Pope Benedict XVI likewise deepened our understanding of the council's teaching, most notably in his motu proprio *Summorum Pontificum*.[26] If we are to be obedient to Vatican II, teaching our faith communities Latin ought to be a priority for pastors, music directors, and catechists.

Now that we know what Vatican II taught about Latin, let's focus on its teachings on the vernacular. The fact is that the majority of Catholics at this point are familiar with the liturgy in their native language. The council states that the vernacular may be used at certain points of the liturgy, but it is not required (*SSC* 36). Specifically, the council makes provision for using the native tongue of the faith community for the readings of the Mass and the "common prayer," also known as "the prayers of the faithful" (*SSC* 54).

This was not a new idea. As a matter of fact, the discussion of integrating the vernacular into the sacred liturgy was already in progress at the Council of Trent, four centuries before Vatican II. At that time, the Church discerned to maintain the liturgy solely in Latin, no doubt to preserve the unique identity of the Roman liturgy in the face of the Protestant Reformation.

That being said, the use of the vernacular has borne great fruit in the lives of the faithful, especially in acquainting people with the vocabulary of the liturgy. There is something special about praying in your native language. It provides a sense of familiarity.

Ideally, the Mass should make use of both Latin and the vernacular. For example, the proper parts of the Mass such as the Eucharistic Prayer and its responses would be in Latin, whereas the readings, homily, and prayers of the faithful would be in the vernacular. Best of both worlds. At those moments when the priest and people are directly sharing in Christ's adoration of the Father, they speak the universal language of the Church. When they are speaking and reflecting on the mystery as a local community, then they speak in the vernacular. Such a practice simultaneously captures the particularity and universality of the liturgy. For the Mass is both of a particular people and of the universal Church. It is something in our midst as well as something that transcends our own boundaries.

The council was clear in its desire to maintain Latin in the liturgy. It also supported utilizing the vernacular in certain circumstances to the advantage of the local community. Latin and the vernacular do not have to be opposed to one another. They can coexist. Thoughtfully blending Latin and the vernacular as described above would not only take us closer to Vatican II's teachings, but also profoundly deepen our experience of the liturgy itself.

Other Important Reforms

There is much that can be said about Vatican II's reforms outside the celebration of the Eucharist. The focus of this book, however, is not to provide a commentary on every reform of Vatican II, but to highlight false narratives about the council from either the paracouncil or the traditionalists, and to introduce the reader to the theological background of the four major documents. Nonetheless, it is worth mentioning in passing several significant reforms that often go unappreciated.

Expanding Scripture Engagement

In my opinion, one of the best reforms of Vatican II was the reorganization of the readings we use for Mass: "The treasures of the bible are to be opened up more lavishly, so that richer fare may be provided for the faithful at the table of God's word. In this way a more representative portion of the holy scriptures will be read to the people in the course of a prescribed number of years" (*SSC* 51). As I mentioned earlier, the century leading up to the Second Vatican Council saw a revival in scripture scholarship. The council wished to share the gifts of the Church's labors with the faithful and afford them the opportunity to hear more selections from the Bible.

Before Vatican II, the readings used for Mass were dispersed in a single cycle that repeated each year. The council decided to expand this cycle. The finished product was a three-year cycle of readings for Sundays and a two-year cycle of readings for weekdays.

In the cycle of Sunday readings, each year is dedicated to one of the three synoptic gospels: Matthew, Mark, and Luke. The Gospel of John is interspersed throughout the three-year cycle for certain solemnities and Sundays.

The integration of more scriptural texts in the sacred liturgy affords the People of God an opportunity to hear the full story of salvation history. Over a three-year period, the faithful are exposed to large sections of the Bible. Likewise, the expanded variety of readings allows preachers to elaborate on the mysteries of our faith, thus enriching the spirituality of the parish community. I often hear Catholics compare our liturgies to those of our Protestant brothers and sisters. They will make mention of the Protestant focus on sacred scripture, saying that we as Catholics should do more to study the Bible. Vatican II agrees. That is why it reformed the lectionary cycle. The council also encouraged regular celebrations of the Liturgy of the Word: "Bible services [Liturgy of the Word] should be encouraged, especially on the vigils of the more solemn feasts, on some weekdays in Advent and Lent, and on Sundays and feast days" (*SSC* 35). The council aspires to foster a deeper love in the hearts of the faithful for sacred scripture. The reform of the lectionary cycle was one of the primary ways of reaching toward this ideal.

Promoting Preaching

The Mass is composed of two parts: the Liturgy of the Word and the Liturgy of the Eucharist. Keeping in line with its intention to inspire an appreciation for sacred scripture, Vatican II highlights the significance of the Liturgy of the Word and its role in ensuring a fuller celebration of the Eucharist. The council also speaks about the need for preaching. This is yet another admirable and often forgotten aspect of Vatican II's liturgical reform. It elevates the dignity of the homily and even goes so far as to say that preaching is an integral part of the liturgy itself. "In fact, at those Masses which are celebrated on Sundays and holydays of obligation, with the people assisting, it [the homily] should not be omitted except for a serious reason" (*SSC* 52).

By and large, we are on the right track in regard to Vatican II's vision for preaching. Most priests agree that the homily is vital to our Eucharistic celebrations. Preaching at daily Mass as well as on Sundays is a staple in most parishes nowadays. That was not the case before Vatican II. But now, preaching is a routine part of the liturgy. Likewise, seminaries are striving to provide solid homiletical formation for our future priests so that they might more readily instruct the faithful about sacred scripture and inspire holiness. Pope Francis, building on the teachings of Vatican II, summarizes the importance of the homily in his encyclical *Evangelii Gaudium*:

> The homily is the touchstone for judging a pastor's closeness and ability to communicate to his people. We know that the faithful attach great importance to it, and that both they and their ordained ministers suffer because of homilies: the laity from having to listen to them and the clergy from having to preach them! It is sad that this is the case. The homily can actually be an intense and happy experience of the Spirit, a consoling encounter with God's word, a constant source of renewal and growth. Let us renew our confidence in preaching, based on the conviction that it is God who seeks to reach out to others through the preacher, and that he displays his power through human words.[27]

Pope Francis's blunt assessment of the homily's importance in the sacred liturgy highlights the reality that good homilies can greatly influence the congregation's experience of the Holy Eucharist. Personally, I have found the homily to be among the most effective methods of conversion for a parish community. It is a prime opportunity to catechize, inspire, and form souls.

My first parish assignment after ordination was to a community desiring spiritual and catechetical formation. After nearly two decades of lackluster liturgies, few sacraments, and stale preaching, they were hungering for renewal. The new pastor and I decided to pour our energy into two things: the beauty of the liturgy and good preaching.

God blessed the endeavor. In less than three years, weekly Mass attendance rose from six hundred people to nearly a thousand. Many of these newcomers were young families. Every weekend we saw new faces. When we asked them why they started attending St. Mary, the response was unanimous: "Father, the liturgies are so beautiful and we love the homilies." It's no exaggeration to say that good liturgy and preaching saved St. Mary Catholic Church and School. With newfound energy filling the hearts of our parishioners, we were able to start ministries, fund projects, renovate buildings, and feed the poor—all because we trusted in the power of Christ's liturgy.

There is no need to reinvent the wheel. Jesus gave us all that we need to inspire souls and bring them back to the Church. One of the most powerful weapons in our pastoral arsenal is passionate preaching guided by the three-year lectionary cycle of Vatican II.

Revising the Liturgical Calendar

Another important reform of Vatican II was the restructuring of the liturgical calendar—the annual seasons and solemnities of the Church. The council wanted to refocus the annual celebrations of the liturgy to more perfectly convey the whole mystery of Christ's life.

In the centuries leading up to Vatican II, several problematic customs had developed in regard to liturgical celebrations, most notably the veneration of saints or local patrons in a manner that overshadowed or displaced the fundamental events of salvation itself. Addressing this issue directly, the council made it clear that "lest the feasts of the saints should take precedence over the feasts which commemorate the very mysteries of salvation, many of them should be left to be celebrated by a particular Church or nation or family of religious; only those should be extended to the universal Church which commemorate saints who are truly of universal importance" (*SSC* 111). This is to be observed in a special way on Sundays: "The Lord's Day is the original feast day. . . . Other celebrations, unless they be truly of greatest importance, shall not have precedence over the Sunday which is the foundation and kernel of the whole liturgical year" (*SSC* 106).

Vatican II's revision of the liturgical calendar built on reforms that were already underway. In 1955, Pope Pius XII had reorganized the Holy Week celebrations. Most significantly, he reformed the Easter Vigil, which, for all intents and purposes, had become a blip on the liturgical radar. Returning to the ancient Church's teachings, Pope Pius XII reestablished the Easter Vigil as the most solemn celebration of the entire liturgical calendar and gave it a renewed status in the liturgical life of the Church. Vatican II continued the reforms begun by Pius XII, reiterating the dignity of Sunday above and beyond the celebrations of local saints or traditional holidays. The Council also simplified the calendar to make it more streamlined and rhythmic as it cycles through the core mysteries of our salvation, especially the Nativity and the Paschal Mystery, which constitute the hinges of the liturgical year.

Renewing the Initiation of Adults into the Church

Another landmark reform of Vatican II is the Rite of Christian Initiation of Adults (RCIA). This is the program used when people who are not Catholic want to be received into full communion with the Catholic Church. The council asked for a complete overhaul of the RCIA. In so doing, the council mandated a return to the ancient process of the catechumenate in which those desiring to become Christians undergo a formation composed of four stages:

Precatechumenate, Catechumenate, Initiation, and Mystagogy. This remains one of the great reforms of the Second Vatican Council. Sadly, it is often one of the least developed in our parishes.

The council fathers hoped to recapture the original enthusiasm and depth of ancient Christian initiation, but the ball was dropped in the two decades following Vatican II. Now, many RCIA programs simply have candidates take a couple of classes where they watch videos or do a form of Bible study. Usually, the courses lack theological depth and are practically void of liturgical formation in central aspects of Catholic practice, such as how to attend Eucharistic Adoration, pray the Liturgy of the Hours, do lectio divina, or make a good Confession. Instead, the candidates are expected to learn a few prayers and basic teachings of the faith. Some programs become Bible studies with commentary offered by the instructor. Few RCIA programs succeed in immersing the catechumen into the rich tradition and culture of Catholicism.

Where we lack most severely, in my opinion, is in the fourth stage of RCIA, mystagogy. In the ancient Church, mystagogy was the period immediately following a person's initiation into Catholicism. It was a time of further education and accompaniment when the newly initiated person was mentored by another Christian and attended lessons from the clergy about the teachings of the faith. The most famous example from early Catholicism is St. Cyril of Jerusalem's *Mystagogical Catecheses*, a collection of five lectures St. Cyril gave to newly initiated Christians. The lectures address the theology of Baptism, Confirmation, and Holy Communion, as well as a closing lesson on the Mass. Inspired by these and other ancient writings of the Church, the Second Vatican Council wished to reinstate the period of mystagogy as a common practice within dioceses.

The restored RCIA process is a splendid and much-needed reform from Vatican II. Yet, there remains a lot to be done to fully realize it. Renewing our RCIA programs would prove immensely beneficial and sanctifying for the universal Church.

The Divine Office: A Forgotten Treasure

Traditionalists accuse the Second Vatican Council of secularizing or despiritualizing the Church—but we've been discovering that nothing could be further from the truth. At every step, Vatican II sought to give the Church the enthusiasm and tools necessary to evangelize the world and sanctify the People of God—and this impulse is on full display in the council's writings on the Divine Office, also called the Liturgy of the Hours.

The Divine Office is an official form of prayer consisting of a series of readings and intercessions on behalf of the Church. At the heart of the Liturgy of the Hours is the psalmody, a collection of psalms recited throughout the day. Technically, the Divine Office is the highest form of liturgy besides the Mass. In fact, it is an extension of the Mass, a continuation of the praise offered to God through the sacrifice of Christ in the Eucharist. The council describes it in the following way:

> By tradition going back to early Christian times, the divine office is devised so that the whole course of the day and night is made holy by the praises of God. Therefore, when this wonderful song of praise is rightly performed by priests and others who are deputed for this purpose by the Church's ordinance, or by the faithful praying together with the priest in the approved form, then it is truly the voice of the bride addressed to her bridegroom; it is the very prayer which Christ Himself, together with His body, addresses to the Father. Hence all who render this service are not only fulfilling a duty of the Church, but also are sharing in the greatest honor of Christ's spouse, for by offering these praises to God they are standing before God's throne in the name of the Church their Mother. (*SSC* 84)

Praying the psalms is a practice that goes back to the Jewish people, who prayed three times a day in recognition of God's presence and goodness. The ancient Church continued a version of this practice. St. Benedict solidified a routine of prayer called the diurnal office or canonical hours, which included seven different times of recitation: Matins/Lauds, Prime, Terce, Sext, None, Vespers, and Compline. This has been a staple of monastic and clerical life ever since. It is one way the Church remains faithful to the exhortation of St. Paul: "Pray without ceasing" (1 Thes 5:17).

The Second Vatican Council continued the work started in 1911 by St. Pius X, cementing several reforms to the Divine Office. Reasons for the changes abounded, but basically the council wanted to restore the original intention of the Liturgy of the Hours, which had become somewhat skewed by the 1950s. Instead of praying the hours at their prescribed times, some priests had gotten into the habit of saying all the hours in one fell swoop at the end of the day. Some even said hours prescribed for the following day the night before. The Divine Office was perceived more as a chore than a blessing. Part of the reason these bad habits developed was that the structure of the Divine Office was not tenable for the busyness of parish life. The breviary was organized in accord with a monastic mentality, not taking into account the busy schedules of priests and religious engaged in apostolic work.

Vatican II remedied both the situation of spiritual laxity and the need for practicality in a couple ways. First, the one-week cycle of psalms was made into a four-week cycle. The daily prayers were streamlined to include a hymn, three psalms, one reading, the responsory, and the closing prayer. The hinge hours of Lauds and Vespers included the Canticle of Zechariah and the Canticle of Mary, respectively, along with intercessions. In keeping with the goal to integrate works by the Church Fathers in the daily life of the Church, the Office of Readings—traditionally called Matins—was expanded so as to provide a richer selection of patristic writings.

The Office of Readings was also revised to include more readings from sacred scripture that synced with the newly revised three-year lectionary cycle.

Second, the council stated that priests and religious not living in a cloistered community were not bound to pray all seven hours of the breviary. Rather, they were vowed to pray the Office of Readings, Lauds, Vespers, Compline, and one of the midday prayers of their choice.

I have mentioned some of the technical reforms to the Divine Office. Likewise, much can be said about the value of the Divine Office. But for our purposes, let us discuss one of the great innovations of Vatican II regarding the Liturgy of the Hours, namely, the council's invitation for the laity to actively incorporate it into their daily lives. Before Vatican II, the Divine Office was largely seen as a form of prayer reserved for clergy and religious. In contrast to this mentality, the council asserts that

> Lay people gathering for prayer, apostolic work, or any other reason are encouraged to fulfill the Church's duty, by celebrating part of the liturgy of the hours. The laity must learn above all how in the liturgy they are adoring God the Father in spirit and in truth; they should bear in mind that through public worship and prayer they reach all humanity and can contribute significantly to the salvation of the whole world.[28]

It does not stop there. The council even goes so far as to encourage families to pray the Liturgy of the Hours together at home: "It is of great advantage for the family, the domestic sanctuary of the Church, not only to pray together to God but also to celebrate some parts of the liturgy of the hours as occasion offers, in order to enter more deeply into the life of the Church."[29]

Vatican II draws our hearts to some extraordinarily important realities here, and reminds us of the vital connections between prayer, community, and the Christian life. We do not follow Christ in isolation. We are one body, gathered together by the grace of God. Prayer is not only a private activity, but also a communal affair in which we speak on behalf of our brothers and sisters throughout the world. Every baptized Catholic shares in this duty. There is no better way to enact this sacred obligation than praying the Liturgy of the Hours with our family and friends.

The Liturgy of the Hours is a neglected treasure of the Church. In my experience, many, if not most, Catholics do not even know it exists, highlighting a significant gap in the Church's spiritual formation. As a parish priest, I regularly advise people on their spiritual life. The Divine Office is one of the first things I recommend. If you want to grow in holiness and devotion, start praying the Liturgy of the Hours! This advice translates to parishes as well. If we want holy parishes that are on fire with love for God, start praying the Liturgy of the Hours as a community. There is no better way. No wonder Vatican II decreed it as a pastoral responsibility: "Pastors of souls should see to it that the chief hours, especially Vespers, are celebrated in common in the church on Sundays and the more solemn feasts. And the laity, too, are encouraged to recite the divine office, either with the priests, or among themselves, or even individually" (*SSC* 100).

At my own parish, we started praying the Liturgy of the Hours every Tuesday evening in the context of Eucharistic Adoration. Likewise, we couple the Liturgy of the Hours with major religious functions or liturgies, including penance services, parish missions, Holy Days of Obligation, and the Sacred Triduum. The people of our parish have become so accustomed to it that many of them pray the breviary privately on a daily basis. It is such a joy to see multiple people coming to Mass with a breviary under their arm. Several of our young families gather regularly to pray the breviary in their homes. Now, the Liturgy of the Hours is a regular spiritual practice in the parish.

I do not exaggerate when I say that encouraging the Liturgy of the Hours and providing regular opportunities for it to be practiced completely transformed the culture and spirituality of our parish. It has deepened the prayer life of our people and inspired vocations to the priesthood and religious life. I cannot say enough about the benefits of the Divine Office. Every priest should be working to make the Liturgy of the Hours a staple in the life of his flock, and every layperson should be taking full advantage of praying the breviary as much as possible.

Restoring Beauty: Sacred Music, Sacred Art, and Sacred Furnishings

One day I was teaching my eighth-grade philosophy class about the medieval period. When we arrived at the subject of music, I played a recording of Gregorian chant. As the class listened to the monks singing, I noticed that one of the girls sitting in the second row started to cry. I stopped the recording and asked what was wrong. She responded, "Nothing, Father. I just haven't heard something so beautiful before. Why don't we sing that kind of music at Mass?"

No institution on earth has created or propagated more beauty than the Catholic Church. Indeed, it was the Church that salvaged culture from the ashes of fallen Rome, taking the crumbled columns of the Colosseum and crafting them into the colonnades of St. John Lateran. We built cathedrals, composed symphonies, sculpted masterpieces, and penned epics. This is not triumphalism; it is history. The Second Vatican Council recognized this proud tradition and strived to maintain it:

> The fine arts are considered to rank among the noblest activities of man's genius, and this applies especially to religious art and to its highest achievement, which is sacred art. . . . Holy Mother Church has therefore always been the friend of the fine arts and has ever sought their noble help, with the special aim that all things set

apart for use in divine worship should be truly worthy, becoming, and beautiful, signs and symbols of the supernatural world, and for this purpose she has trained artists. In fact, the Church has, with good reason, always reserved to herself the right to pass judgment upon the arts, deciding which of the works of artists are in accordance with faith, piety, and cherished traditional laws, and thereby fitted for sacred use. (*SSC* 122)

The council fathers saw art as it truly is: a testament to the Incarnation of Jesus and a form of glorifying God. Likewise, they noticed the decline of culture brought on by relativism and deconstructionism. These mentalities create a cold world filled with ugly and illogical things. Looking at a piece of contemporary "art" such as Marcel Duchamp's *Fountain*—which is literally a urinal—or *My Bed*, by Tracey Emin, is proof enough. The standards of art are being degraded and often fall short of their foundational role to point toward the transcendent.

Vatican II saw that the world we live in desperately needs beauty. Ours is a superficial civilization starved for transcendence and substance. If the Church is to save souls, she must lead with beauty and take up once again her rightful place as the arbiter of culture. This is one of the teachings of Vatican II that we have botched horribly. So many church buildings are now mere auditoriums with pews. In some parishes, the music at weekend Mass is hokey and mediocre. Sacred art has all but died away. The glistening towers of stained glass in Notre-Dame Cathedral are but a remnant of the past, replaced in newer church buildings with plain windows and barren, whitewashed walls. What happened? Why did we so readily abandon our history and thousands of years of artistic development?

Trading Beauty for "Relevance"

In the years following the council, unhealthy theologies—propped up by the paracouncil—weaseled their way into liturgical music, sacred art, church architecture, and sacred furnishings. *The music needs to be more inclusive and less theological. The art shouldn't be extravagant; it needs to be humble. Church architecture should remove distractions such as the tabernacle and statues. Sacred furnishings should be simple. After all, Jesus didn't use a gold chalice or wear fancy chasubles!* All of these claims were made under the supposed auspices of Vatican II.

The paracouncil points to two sections in *Sacrosanctum Concilium* as justification for its assertions. First, in paragraph 34, the council states that "the rites [of the liturgy] should be distinguished by a noble simplicity; they should be short, clear, and unencumbered by useless repetitions; they should be within the people's powers of comprehension, and normally should not require much explanation" (*SSC* 34). The phrase "noble simplicity" was—and still is—twisted to suggest that the council wanted the Church to strip itself of the trappings of previous liturgical forms or traditions. According to this thinking, there was a need to return to the bare minimum and remove anything not absolutely essential to the celebration of the liturgy.

The second section is in paragraph 124, in which the council exhorts bishops to "strive after noble beauty rather than mere sumptuous display. This principle is to apply also in the matter of sacred vestments and ornaments" (*SSC* 124). According to the paracouncil's interpretation of this statement, vestments and sacred vessels should be plain and simple—it is "against the spirit of Vatican II" to have ornate vestments or gold chalices.

In its interpretation of both paragraphs 34 and 124, the paracouncil makes the vital mistake of cherry-picking the teachings of Vatican II. For example, in the same section where the council makes its statement about "sumptuous display," it also states that bishops are to "carefully remove from the house of God and from other sacred places those works of artists which are repugnant to faith, morals, and Christian piety, and which offend true religious sense either by depraved forms or by lack of artistic worth, mediocrity and pretense"(*SSC* 124). Likewise, "when churches are to be built, let great care be taken that they be suitable for the celebration of liturgical services and for the active participation of the faithful" (*SSC* 124). Finally, "ordinaries must be very careful to see that sacred furnishings and works of value are not disposed of or dispersed; for they are the ornaments of the house of God" (*SSC* 126). The council is also clear that "noble simplicity" is to be enacted in unison with the sound tradition of Catholicism (*SSC* 23). We can't toss out the baby with the bathwater. Vatican II did not seek to return us to year zero in the life of the Church.

The flawed thinking of the paracouncil had devastating consequences in Catholic culture, and we are now seeing the consequences. Most Catholic youth today cannot sing a single chant or even hum the tune of "Holy God, We Praise Thy Name." They cannot recognize the works of Raphael or Caravaggio. They cannot quote a terza of Dante or recite a passage from Shakespeare. They are unable to point out the tabernacle in the church and do not know the names of the sacred vessels. Yet, they can give you the stats of their favorite basketball team and tell you the handle of a famous gamer. Pop singers' names roll off their tongues, and they can rattle off the usernames of multiple YouTube stars. Yes, the modern world has done a much better job enculturating our children than we have—and it is completely our fault.

We were told that if we became more hip and less outdated, we could compete with the world. All we had to do was abandon our tradition. But the desperate pursuit of relevance has failed, and we are paying the price as droves of young Catholics leave the Church. It is time to stop letting the world give us advice on evangelization!

Reclaiming our tradition of sacred beauty—immediately—is of the utmost pastoral concern.

Reclaiming Sacred Beauty in the Liturgy

If we are going to restore the Church as the arbiter of art and culture (rather than a pale imitation of the world's counterfeits), we must start with the sacred liturgy. And here we can see exactly why the Second Vatican Council includes its commentary on sacred art in its document on the liturgy. The sacraments are the premier site of catechesis and evangelization. This is especially true of the Holy Eucharist. So it stands to reason that the *way* Mass is celebrated is key. This is what Pope Benedict XVI calls the *ars celebrandi* ("art of celebration"). Although it applies primarily to the priest, it can just as easily relate to the entirety of the liturgy and all persons involved. Every gesture and facial expression transmits a message either for or against the reality of Christ's presence in the Holy Eucharist. If we celebrate the Mass or any other sacrament nonchalantly, people will see it as unimportant and inconsequential. Disorganized and unprofessional parishes communicate that they are not worth supporting. Tattered vestments and worn sacred vessels convey that what takes place on the altar does not deserve respect. When ministers of hospitality and extraordinary ministers of Holy Communion show up five minutes before Mass starts, they are communicating that serving Christ is a hobby or a chore, not an honor.

Priests are responsible for setting the right tone. As Fulton J. Sheen said, "Spirituality begins at the top, not at the bottom."[30] The people watch their priest and take their cues from his devotion. "There could be no more fatal error for the priest than to underestimate the sacerdotal dignity. He must on the contrary have a very high conception of it."[31] This is not arrogance; it is reality, the responsibility given to men chosen to live *in persona Christi*. And "in all their apostolic activity, pastors of souls should energetically set about achieving [sacerdotal dignity] through requisite pedagogy."[32]

The council lays out a vision for implementing liturgical reform, namely, the conscious participation of the faithful *through adequate catechesis and liturgical formation by their clergy.* The faith community is only as holy as its priest. A parish is not judged by its funds or the number of its ministries. Souls can still be lost or lukewarm at a parish with a million dollars in the bank. A parish is gauged by the sacredness of its liturgies and the holiness of its pastors. If these two things are in order, everything else will fall into place.

Sacred music also plays a vital role. As a professional musician and the son of a music director, I hold this topic close to my heart. People readily acknowledge the transformative power of music. Songs carry meaning and purpose. They can evoke memory and foster encounter. Music is the most transcendental of all the arts. In a special way, "the musical tradition of the universal Church is a treasure of inestimable value, greater even than that of art" (*SSC* 112). This is why Vatican II commands that the "treasury of sacred music is to be preserved and fostered with great care" (*SSC* 114). Among the many styles of Church music, the "Church recognizes Gregorian chant as being specially suited to the Roman liturgy. Therefore . . . it should be given pride of place in liturgical services" (*SSC* 116).

When it comes to the liturgy, it is not a question of taste or preference. It is a question of suitability. I urge you to ask yourself the same question I raised in our earlier discussion of *ad orientem* and *versus populum*: What most perfectly captures the theology of the Mass? I may like folk music or rock, but my musical preferences don't define good Church music. Likewise, overlaying secular music styles with Christian lyrics does not produce liturgical hymns. Art in the liturgy has a very specific responsibility, namely, to cultivate worship that is oriented toward the sacrifice of the altar. As such, in order for something to be fitting for sacred worship, it must flow from a living encounter with Christ and be informed by the theology and tradition of the Church. It must possess Catholic sentiment, which is to say, an understanding of Catholic tradition and teachings.

It would beneficial for bishops and priests to be more involved in the process of actively forming artists, musicians, architects, and poets in their vocations. We can see an example of this kind of collaboration in the sixteenth and seventeenth centuries, a period that birthed splendid pieces of sacred art. St. Charles Borromeo composed a document for artists detailing the proper ways to apply the decrees of the Council of Trent to the designs and decorations of Catholic churches. The book was so popular that it was reprinted nineteen times![33] St. Charles understood that although an artist may be talented in their craft, the role of preaching, teaching, and catechizing lies squarely on the shoulders of the magisterium. The Church needs to mentor artists, especially young aspiring artists in our Catholic schools and parishes so as to form their hearts in accord with the mind of the Church. Then, these young men and women will produce art for the sacred liturgy that truly participates in the right worship of God and properly fulfills the decrees set by Vatican II.

Let's briefly turn our focus to church architecture. Denis McNamara is one of the leading church architects in the United States. He published a wonderful and informative book entitled *Catholic Church Architecture and the Spirit of the Liturgy*. I strongly encourage you to read it since he goes into more detail than the context of this book allows. However, there are a few points worth mentioning here. First, McNamara notes that one of the main reasons for a slew of theologically incorrect buildings after the Second Vatican Council was a "genuine and good-willed concern for a perceived active participation."[34] He notes that the definition of active participation was shallow, leading to a degradation of liturgical art and architecture in Catholicism. This was coupled with an inadequate understanding of beauty based on personal opinion as opposed to objective truth. Thus, in order to restore beauty in church art and architecture, we need to reexamine the purpose of any church building within its broader theological context: "Since architecture is the built form of ideas, only with proper ideas about the very ontological nature of a church building can one even begin to consider building a proper church, a church that reveals . . . the very reality of its being."[35]

What is the purpose of sacred art, sacred music, and sacred buildings? To reveal the mysteries of the faith. Each does so in its own way, but their mission is the same. They are intended to foster contemplation of the divine mysteries, *in continuity with the art forms of tradition*, so as to allow for a genuine encounter with Jesus Christ in the Holy Eucharist and the other sacraments of the Church.

The Russian writer Dostoevsky boldly declared, "Beauty will save the world." Hans Urs von Balthasar makes a similar claim in *Seeing the Form*, the first volume of his trilogy *The Glory of the Lord*. Balthasar notes that, in a world dominated by empirical reason and cold facts, there is a desperate ache in people's hearts for genuine beauty—not a purely subjective beauty dictated by the eye of the beholder, but an objective beauty that draws us out of ourselves into divine things, one that stirs the deepest recesses of our humanity and orients our hearts to transcendence.

I experience this regularly as a contributor to *Word on Fire*. I first started writing for their blog in response to multiple requests from millennial and Gen Z followers who wanted *Word on Fire* to provide in-depth Catholic commentary on video-game culture. I was tapped to offer philosophical and theological reflections on the phenomenon of video games and their rising popularity. My first article was entitled "Game On: Why Video Games Appeal to the Hungry Heart." I was shocked by the reception. Emails started pouring in from around the world expressing gratitude and excitement. One of my most popular articles is "Video Games: A Lesson on the Importance of Aesthetics," in which I comment on the high priority that tech designers place on the beauty of a video game. One thing the worldwide success of the video-game industry has taught us is the priority and indispensability of beauty. Sometimes Christians forget the power of beauty—especially in the liturgy—and its role in the promotion of the Gospel:

> We would sooner invest $15,000 in a new high-tech sound system or installing projector screens into the sanctuary before thinking of spending half that amount for a statue of the Blessed Mother or a fresco depicting the life of our Lord. The gaming industry does not make the same mistake. . . . As Catholics, we are inheritors of the most prestigious and splendorous beauty in history. Nothing can compare to the haunting neumes of Hildegard's chants and the soaring melodies of Mozart's masses, the epic adventure of Dante's *Divine Comedy* and the stirring speeches of *The Song of Roland*, the stunning architectural feats of Notre Dame cathedral and awe-inspiring brushstrokes of Michelangelo's Sistine Chapel. What is more, we have a story to tell. Not a made-up story about aliens far away or a great battle against magical creatures, but a "true myth" as J. R. R. Tolkien called it—the greatest story ever told. . . . If we were to expose the world to the beautiful tradition of Catholicism and allow this tradition to inform our future decisions in the divine liturgy, sacred arts, architecture, music, and means of evangelization, there would be no need to invent new programs or have workshops. People would flock to Mass and see our parishes as bastions of culture augmenting and conveying the deepest yearnings of the human heart.[36]

As we seek to reclaim Vatican II, a return to the tradition of beauty is vital. This remains one of the main reasons many young people leave the Catholic Church for traditionalist sects such as the SSPX. They are struck by the beauty and solemnity of these traditionalist celebrations. Some people critique these Catholics, calling their faith shallow or obsessed with pomp and circumstance. But it is often a lot more than that. Perhaps their decision to leave their local parish is incorrect, but their desire for beauty is not.

We have a pastoral and evangelical obligation to beautify our churches. It is not simply superficial or peripheral. It is essential. For this reason, the Code of Canon Law asserts that the proper ordering of divine worship is the first purpose of the Church's acquisition of temporal goods.[37] In other words, the main reason the Church acquires money and resources is to ensure the dignity of the sacred liturgy so that "from the rising of the sun to its setting let the name of the LORD be praised" (Ps 113:3).

I firmly believe—and have experienced in my own ministry—that Vatican II provides us with a clear, life-giving vision of what the sacred liturgy is, one that can enrich and renew our faith communities. This theologically robust vision can guide the types of practices we choose and where we decide to spend our pastoral energies. Absorbing more deeply Vatican II's teachings on the sacred liturgy will foster active participation in the genuine sense of the term, revive the power and beauty of tradition in today's context, and ultimately renew the joyful and wondrous task at the heart of the Church's calling—the task of drawing all creation into a right and proper worship of God.

4

THE CHURCH

The Second Vatican Council is often referred to as the Council of the Church. Its Dogmatic Constitution on the Church, *Lumen Gentium*, is considered its crowning jewel—it represents nearly two hundred years of development in the field of ecclesiology, the theological discipline that studies the nature and origins of the Church.

Due to the discovery of numerous patristic texts, ecclesiology experienced a revival during the nineteenth and twentieth centuries. Among the first major figures in this revival was a German priest named Johann Adam Möhler. Möhler gained esteem in his early years of priesthood when, at the age of twenty-seven, he challenged the prestigious faculty at the University of Freiburg, who were pushing to remove celibacy from the priesthood. His trenchant defense of priestly celibacy, entitled *Illumination on a Memorandum concerning the Elimination of Celibacy Prescribed for Catholic Priests*, debunked the shallow claims of the university staff and led to a renewal of vocations to the priesthood throughout Europe. Having established himself as a stellar theologian, Möhler went on to publish several landmark works dealing with the nature of the Church.

Among Möhler's most famous works is *Unity in the Church*, a book that reflects on the ecclesiology of the first three centuries of

Catholicism. Even though this book was published in 1825, we can already see ideas developing that would come into full blossom at Vatican II. The Church as a pilgrim people, the unity of the Church as Christ's Mystical Body, the universal nature of the Church, the role of the hierarchy and laity—all these themes were discussed by Möhler and later refined by the Second Vatican Council.

St. John Henry Newman followed in Möhler's footsteps with his classic work *An Essay on the Development of Christian Doctrine*, in which the ecclesiological themes initially explored by Möhler begin to mature. Drawing on a wide range of patristic resources, from Origen and Clement to Hippolytus and Eusebius, St. Newman delivered a comprehensive survey of ecclesiological development in history.

Small wonder that *Lumen Gentium*, building as it does on so many decades of rich scholarship, is noted for its tremendous influence and spiritual depth. That being said, *Lumen Gentium* remains largely undiscussed in the wider Church. In particular, the document's chapter on the Blessed Virgin Mary and her relation to the Church remains one of the unmined gems of Vatican II.

Our reflection on *Lumen Gentium* will follow the outline of the document itself. We will begin with the council's definition of the Church, focusing on the Church as the People of God. This will lead to a brief discussion of one of the major themes of *Lumen Gentium*: the universal call to holiness. Finally, we will end with the Church as a pilgrim people and her relationship with the Blessed Virgin Mary. As usual, throughout the chapter, we will address different ways the paracouncil and traditionalism have twisted *Lumen Gentium* or misinterpreted its teachings.

The Church according to Vatican II: The Sacrament of Salvation

When I say the word "church," what comes to mind? People give many answers to this question—a building, a community, a denomination. Vatican II gives one answer: The Church is the sacrament of salvation (*LG* 48). There are many different ways to express this: the Church as Bride of Christ, Mystical Body, People of God, and so on. But, in the end, the Church is a sacrament. She is a visible sign of an invisible reality:

> Since the Church is in Christ like a sacrament or as a sign and instrument both of a very closely knit union with God and of the unity of the whole human race, it desires now to unfold more fully to the faithful of the Church and to the whole world its own inner nature and universal mission. (*LG* 1)

The Church as a Sacrament of the Triune God

The council goes on to explain that the Church is a sacrament of the unity of the Blessed Trinity. We can see this in the process of salvation history and the revelation of the divine persons in and through that history.

God the Father willed creation into being, blessing it with a plan for communion that reflected in a creaturely way the perfect communion of the Trinity. Even though Adam sinned, God did not abandon his will for communion, but established a covenant with Israel, which became a precursor to the Church. All of the covenants and prophecies God made with the Jewish people pointed to and prepared the way for the ultimate covenant and prophecy to be fulfilled in Jesus Christ. Thus, the letter to the Hebrews claims, "In times past, God spoke in partial and various ways to our ancestors through the prophets; in these last days, he spoke to us through a son, whom he made heir of all things and through whom he created the universe" (Heb 1:1–2).

The Son is sent from the Father to establish a new people, not just among Israel but a universal kingdom that will include all those who seek the truth: "I have other sheep that do not belong to this fold. These also I must lead, and they will hear my voice, and there will be one flock, one shepherd" (Jn 10:16). From the very beginning of his public ministry Christ gathers a community unto himself, calling them to "repent, and believe in the gospel" (Mk 1:15). These three words from Mark are key to understanding Christ's mission: *metanoeite*, "repent"; *pisteuete*, "believe"; and *euangeliō*, "the gospel." *Metanoeite* and *pisteuete* are inherently connected and necessitate a personal commitment beyond intellectual consent.[1] Christianity is more than mere agreement or acceptance. A true act of Christian faith (*pisteuete*) can only take place with a sincere conversion (*metanoeite*) of heart fully committed to loving Jesus. It is not enough to say, "I believe in what Christianity teaches." We must believe in *him*.

This brings us to *euangeliō*, the Gospel. What is the Gospel? Is it a book? Is it a set of sayings and teachings? No. It is Jesus Christ himself. In Christ there is no separation between the speaker and the spoken. The proclaimer and the proclaimed are essentially the same. He is not a third-party messenger sent to announce something outside himself like Muhammad or Buddha; it is Jesus Christ himself who is the message. Jesus is the Word (see John 1:1). He is the mission of God. He is "the way and the truth and the life" (Jn 14:6). Christianity is not an abstract religion. It is not an ethical program or moral protocol. It is an incarnate faith that requires a living relationship. To be a Christian does not mean to follow Christ, it means to *be* Christ; to share in his very life: "For all of you who were baptized into Christ have clothed yourselves with Christ" (Gal 3:27) and "Yet I live, no longer I, but Christ lives in me" (Gal 2:20).

Those who enter into this relationship become citizens of the kingdom of God, that is, the Church. For the kingdom is not a faraway place or a fantasyland we go to when we die. People will not say "'Look, here it is,' or, 'There it is.' For behold, the kingdom of God is among you" (Lk 17:21). The Church is the kingdom of

God, the place where we find communion with the Lord and a foretaste of that perfect union we will experience in heaven. It is the sacrament that will never pass away and abides faithfully in the world until all things are fulfilled in Christ. Or, as *Lumen Gentium* so succinctly puts it, "The Church is the kingdom of Christ already present in mystery" (*LG* 3).

The Catholic Church, therefore, is not an accident of history or an invention of later Christian communities. Rather, founding the Church is the express intention of the Incarnation. Catholicism is God's will realized in the world. The Church is the way by which Christ continues to adore the Father and dwell in our midst. "As often as the sacrifice of the cross in which Christ our Passover was sacrificed, is celebrated on the altar, the work of our redemption is carried on" (*LG* 3). Only in light of this fact do the words of the Great Commission make sense: "Behold, I am with you always, until the end of the age" (Mt 28:20). The Church is the way Christ remains with us until the end. Thus, we cannot experience Christ fully without the Church, and the more "we *live* internally in her and she in us, so much more alive is the conviction from Christ manifested in us and from it what he is and is to be for us."[2]

When the Son completes his work by creating the Church from the blood and water that flowed from his pierced side on the Cross, he opens the door for the Holy Spirit to enter the hearts of the faithful and inspire the soul of the Church. By the Spirit's grace, the Church is continually sanctified and bonded into a perfect unity of love that crosses the boundaries of space and time.

Here is yet another area that Vatican II enriched—the understanding of the Holy Spirit's role in the life of the Church. A priest named Fr. Yves Congar was instrumental in this development. Congar emerged in the 1950s as a leading scholar in the field of pneumatology, which is the study of the Holy Spirit. His book *I Believe in the Holy Spirit* remains one of the milestone works of the twentieth century. Drawing on the writings of the Church Fathers, especially St. Basil the Great, Congar had tremendous influence on *Lumen Gentium,* especially with his insights about the role of the Holy Spirit as the active agent of communion in the Church.

Congar notes that the Holy Spirit, as person, is the communion of the Father and Son. He is the love that binds the Father and the Son, and their mutual gift to one another. To be a Christian means to be drawn into this loving communion, even "becoming 'communion' and thus entering into the mode of existence of the Holy Spirit"—to be gift.[3] Thus, St. Paul says that "the love of God has been poured out into our hearts through the holy Spirit that has been given to us" (Rom 5:5). "Hence, the Church has been seen as 'a people made one with the unity of the Father, the Son and the Holy Spirit'" (*LG* 4). She is the sacrament of the unity of the Trinity, bound together by the love of the Holy Spirit.

The Sole Church of Christ

Given the Catholic Church's identity as the sacrament of the unity of the Trinity, in which human beings are drawn into God's communion of love, it stands to reason that the Catholic Church is the sole church of Christ. "This Church constituted and organized in the world as a society, subsists in the Catholic Church, which is governed by the successor of Peter and by the Bishops in communion with him" (*LG* 8). St. Cyprian of Carthage makes the point well in his letters on the Church:

> God is one and Christ one, the Church one, and the Chair founded on Peter by the voice of the Lord is one. It is not possible to found another altar nor create a new priesthood against the one altar and the one priesthood. Whoever gathers elsewhere scatters.[4]

The paracouncil downplayed this understanding of the Catholic Church, seeing it as too exclusive. There was a tendency to soften the boundaries and distinctions between the Catholic Church and the secular world, under the misguided belief that doing so would help people outside the Church find her more approachable and relatable.

One such example was given in chapter 1 when we spoke about Edward Schillebeeckx and his claim that Vatican II defined the Church as the "sacrament of the world" in contrast to the council's actual definition of the Church as the "sacrament of salvation." Schillebeeckx's assertion disregards the uniqueness of the Church in the world and her special role to remind the world what it is called to be. The Church is not supposed to conform to the world, nor is the world in and of itself the sacrament of Christ's saving action. Rather, the Church is made up of those people who have been set apart and consecrated within the world, but who are not of the world (see John 17:16–17).

In the same vein, the paracouncil negatively affected Vatican II's endeavors in the area of ecumenism, the cooperation and unification of Christian communities not in full communion with the Catholic Church. In its document on ecumenism, *Unitatis Redintegratio*, the council was adamant that all the Catholic faithful recognize the signs of the times and take an "active and intelligent part in the work of ecumenism" (*UR* 4)—but not in the manner implemented by the paracouncil.

In the years following Vatican II, in an attempt to be more inclusive of other Christian denominations, it was common for those formed in the mindset of the paracouncil to suppress clear lines of delineation between Catholics and Protestants, particularly in the sacred liturgy. This kind of thinking led to a series of liturgical abuses and ecumenical malpractices, such as allowing Protestant ministers to concelebrate the Eucharistic liturgy or giving non-Catholics Holy Communion. St. John Paul II discussed the danger in his encyclical *Ecclesia de Eucharistia*:

> This has led here and there to ecumenical initiatives
> which, albeit well-intentioned, indulge in Eucharistic

practices contrary to the discipline by which the Church expresses her faith. How can we not express profound grief at all this? The Eucharist is too great a gift to tolerate ambiguity and depreciation. . . . Any such concelebration would not be a valid means, and might well prove instead to be *an obstacle, to the attainment of full communion,* by weakening the sense of how far we remain from this goal and by introducing or exacerbating ambiguities with regard to one or another truth of the faith. The path towards full unity can only be undertaken in truth.[5]

The council's desire for ecumenism is not meant to come at the cost of the Catholic Church's unique character. As the council clearly states:

Our separated brethren, whether considered as individuals or as Communities and Churches, are not blessed with that unity which Jesus Christ wished to bestow on all those who through Him were born again into one body, and with Him quickened to newness of life—that unity which the Holy Scriptures and the ancient Tradition of the Church proclaim. For it is only through Christ's Catholic Church, which is "the all-embracing means of salvation," that they can benefit fully from the means of salvation. . . .

At the same time, the Spirit of Christ has not refrained from using them [other churches and faith communities] as means of salvation which derive their efficacy from the very fullness of grace and truth entrusted to the Church. (*UR* 3)

So what is the council's vision for ecumenism? Vatican II provides four guiding principles for proper ecumenism: (1) genuine assessments of separated denominations' faith, devoid of prejudice or bias, (2) dialogue between competent experts from different churches and faith communities about specific theological issues, (3) cooperation between various Christian denominations for the promotion of the common good, and (4) examination of our faithfulness to Christ and his will for the unity of the Church (*UR* 4). By recognizing the seeds of the Catholic faith present in other Christian denominations, we are meant to build on them in mutual fraternity. As such, we open doors of friendship with our separated brethren, which can hopefully lead to full communion with the Catholic Church.

Truth is the basis of communion. The key to ecumenism is found neither in masking our Catholicism nor in being triumphalist about it, but in letting Catholicism's full splendor shine forth. "You are the light of the world. A city set on a mountain cannot be hidden. Nor do they light a lamp and then put it under a bushel basket; it is set on a lampstand, where it gives light to all in the house. Just so, your light must shine before others" (Mt 5:14–16). The council fathers declared that Christ is the light and that this light burns brightly on the countenance of the Church (*LG* 1). This is clearly indicated by the name of the document on the Church: *Lumen Gentium*, "Light of the Nations."

Another hotly contested topic worth mentioning in this regard is the council's writings in paragraphs 14–16 of *Lumen Gentium*, which teach about the ways in which Catholics are both separate from and also unified with non-Catholic Christians (*LG* 15) and those who have "not yet received the Gospel" (*LG* 16). The discussion is nuanced and deserves much more detail than I can provide in this book. However, it is important to highlight because both the paracouncil and traditionalism misinterpret the council's teachings in these paragraphs. On the one hand, the paracouncil uses Vatican II as an opportunity to deemphasize the Church's nature in an attempt to make her more relatable with the modern world and other Christian denominations. On the other hand, traditionalists often accuse the council of minimizing the importance of the Church and the need for salvation. Some even say Vatican II taught that salvation is possible apart from the Church, rendering the Church irrelevant and her missionary activity unnecessary. Both paraconciliar thinkers and traditionalists use paragraphs 14 through 16 of *Lumen Gentium* to support opposing ideas about salvation.

That being said, the council does not advocate any sort of triumphalist or superior attitude toward our separated brethren. This is where traditionalism tends to fall into error. There is sometimes a mean-spirited, even adversarial sentiment directed toward Protestantism and other non-Catholic communities. That is never the way Catholics should respond to conflict.

True ecumenism is not the conglomeration of many creeds, but the unity of all peoples under a single creed. To be ecumenical does not mean accepting multiple beliefs in Christ, but rather striving to share the same faith in the way Christ revealed it to us. All this must be done in a spirit of peace and mutual fraternity—and it can only be accomplished by a stalwart commitment to the truth, accompanied by a persevering charity.

The Church is not only the sacrament of the Blessed Trinity's unity, but also the sacrament of unity among peoples. She is a sign of the unifying and universal character of Christ's salvation. Likewise, she is the instrument through which Christ gathers his people and calls them to holiness. That leads us to our next topic.

The People of God and the Universal Call to Holiness

Now we arrive at the heart of *Lumen Gentium*. No other council in Church history reflects on the nature and role of the People of God as deeply as the Second Vatican Council. As I mentioned before, the council builds on several centuries of scholarship inspired by a lively reengagement with the Church Fathers. Thus, the notions presented in *Lumen Gentium* revitalize aspects of ecclesiology that had been largely neglected for many centuries. One such notion is the People of God.

There was a propensity after Vatican II to use the phrase "the People of God" to describe the laity. However, when the council refers to "the People of God," it is speaking of all the baptized: clergy, religious, and laity. "What became a typical post-conciliar [paraconciliar] journalist's habit of calling the laity the 'People of God' is without foundation in the conciliar texts."[6] The People of God includes all those who have been incorporated into the Body of Christ and are now on their journey of holiness.

The Church's identity as the People of God can be seen in seminal form in the Old Testament through the Chosen People of Israel. "As Israel according to the flesh, which wandered as an exile in the desert, was already called the Church of God, so too the new Israel which while living in this present age goes in search of a future and abiding city is called the Church of Christ" (*LG* 9). Every event that transpires with the Jewish nation is a harbinger of what will be fulfilled in Christ and the Church.

The first Christians drew these correlations. Origen read the story of Abraham and Isaac as a symbol of Christ's journey to Calvary. St. John Chrysostom interpreted the lamb's blood used in the Passover of Exodus as prefiguring the Holy Eucharist. The Reproaches chanted for the Good Friday liturgy are especially stirring and represent some of the oldest extant hymnody of the Church. They are a collection of calls and responses capturing a dialogue between Christ crucified and the Church:

> My people, what have I done to you?
> Or how have I grieved you? Answer me!
>
> Because I led you out of the land of Egypt,
> You have prepared a Cross for your Savior
>
> I opened the sea before you
> And you opened my side with a lance

I fed you with manna from the desert
And on me you rained blows and lashes.[7]

In the judgment and Crucifixion, Jesus takes the rejection of Israel and redeems it within himself as acceptance and reconciliation. "The people who walked in darkness have seen a great light" (Is 9:1). Christ transforms the darkness of hatred into the light of divine mercy. His sacrifice engenders a new people within his own flesh, a people that he himself will govern. From his pierced side, Christ forms the Church as is so powerfully preached by St. John Chrysostom: "*There flowed from his side water and blood.* . . . Since the symbols of baptism and the eucharist flowed from his side, it was from his side that Christ fashioned the Church, as he had fashioned Eve from the side of Adam."[8] In his Resurrection and Ascension, Christ is established as the cornerstone of the new creation, a chosen people built on solid rock (see Ephesians 2:20; Matthew 7:24).

The Common Priesthood of the Faithful

Thus far, we have summarized the basic teachings of paragraphs 1 through 9 in *Lumen Gentium*. Paragraph 10 introduces a beautiful concept from the Church Fathers that merits special attention, namely, the common priesthood of the faithful. Typically, when we think of a priest, we imagine an ordained person. This is not wrong, but it misses out on the broader notion of priesthood as understood in the ancient Church. To guide our reflection, let us turn to the wisdom of our first pope, St. Peter.

We read in the first letter of St. Peter, "You are 'a chosen race, a royal priesthood, a holy nation, a people of his own, so that you may announce the praises' of him who called you out of darkness into his wonderful light. Once you were 'no people' but now you are God's people" (1 Pt 2:9–10). St. Peter ties his designation of Christians as "a chosen race" and "royal priesthood" to their identity as "God's people." Thus, there is a direct connection between being the People of God and being priests.

After receiving Baptism, every new Christian is anointed on the head with sacred chrism oil while the priest or deacon says, "As Christ was anointed Priest, Prophet, and King, so may you live always as a member of his body, sharing everlasting life." Being a Christian means sharing in the life of Christ—including his ministry of priesthood. To appreciate this, however, we must ask, "What does a priest do?" St. Paul gives us the answer: "I urge you therefore . . . to offer your bodies as a living sacrifice, holy and pleasing to God, your spiritual worship" (Rom 12:1). Sacrificial worship is the principal responsibility of the priesthood. "Sacrifice" is composed of two Latin words: *sacra*, meaning "holy," and *facere*, meaning "to make." Thus, our priestly duty as men and women baptized into Christ is to make ourselves holy and in turn to sanctify the world. That is how we render proper worship to God. This is the same kind of worship Jesus offers to the Father, the worship of his very life. The Second Vatican Council synthesizes this teaching as follows:

> Christ the Lord, High Priest taken from among men, made the new people "a kingdom and priests to God the Father." The baptized, by regeneration and the anointing of the Holy Spirit, are consecrated as a spiritual house and a holy priesthood, in order that through all those works which are those of the Christian man they may offer spiritual sacrifices and proclaim the power of Him who has called them out of darkness into His marvelous light. Therefore, all the disciples of Christ, persevering in prayer and praising God, should present themselves as a living sacrifice, holy and pleasing to God. Everywhere on earth they must bear witness to Christ and give an answer to those who seek an account of that hope of eternal life which is in them. (*LG* 10)

To be God's people is to be a priestly people anointed for a mission of sanctification.

The paracouncil used this language of the common priest-hood to downplay the uniqueness of ordained priesthood. It wasn't unusual in the decades following the council to hear theologians say there was no longer any distinction between the laity and clergy. Rather, the priest's role, they claimed, was purely functional. He was a placeholder representing the community but did not possess any special sacramental character beyond that of the average layperson.

Such mindsets opened the door for a number of liturgical abus-es that are still hurting the Church. It was not unusual to attend a Mass where the laity stood around the altar in a circle and "concele-brated" with the priest. I once spoke with a group of nuns who said they consecrated a loaf of bread on multiple occasions without a priest. Their chaplain assured them that their common priesthood was sufficient to confect the Holy Eucharist. Nowhere do we see greater effect from this tragedy than in the loss of vocations to the priesthood. The sacramental character of the priesthood was assaulted and degraded. Add to this the shame of the sexual abuse crisis in recent years—which no doubt was influenced by the loss of priestly identity—and men cease to think actively about the priesthood. What is attractive about nothing? No one wants to be a placeholder or figurehead. Leading a community in prayer or giving good sermons is not why a man becomes a priest. Those activities will not stir his heart to share in the priesthood of Jesus Christ. He needs to encounter the true essence of the priesthood, the joy and solemn responsibility of being a man chosen among many to provide a distinct ministry within the Church.

Traditionalism responded to the paracouncil's exploitation of the common priesthood by running to the other extreme, emphati-cally asserting the role of the priest while disregarding the council's writings on the laity's ministry of sanctification. As a result, the treasure of Vatican II's reflections on the common priesthood are overshadowed by the paracouncil's hijacking of the Council's theology.

The Second Vatican Council is clear in its desire to both high-light the truth of the common priesthood and simultaneously defend the dignity of the ordained priesthood:

> Though they differ from one another in essence and not only in degree, the common priesthood of the faithful and the ministerial or hierarchical priesthood are nonetheless interrelated: each of them in its own special way is a participation in the one priesthood of Christ. (*LG* 10)

The common priesthood of the faithful and the ordained priest-hood are not opposed to one another. In reality, they are coopera-tive, inspiring one another and building one another up. I can attest to this fact from personal experience. There are few things more life-giving than a holy friendship between a layperson and a priest. We are mirrors to each other, mutually reflecting the holiness to which we have been called and reminding one another of our vocation. Through my ordained ministry, the layperson receives the grace necessary for his or her own ministry of self-sanctifica-tion and that of the world around them. Likewise, they are called to attend to the world in a way I cannot. I have been set apart for the sake of liturgical worship and sacramental care of souls. As much as I would like to be constantly in places of business, public schools, and hospitals preaching the Gospel, it is not possible, nor is it where I belong. I know my place, and I love it. The same is true of a holy layperson. They are well aware of their role in the life of the Church: to be nourished, formed, and inspired by the clergy so as to go out and rise "within the world like leaven" (*LG* 31). St. John Paul II offers a lucid summary in his encyclical dedicated to the laity, *Christifideles Laici*:

> *The "world" thus becomes the place and the means for the lay faithful to fulfill their Christian vocation*, because the world itself is destined to glorify God the Father in

> Christ. The Council is able then to indicate the proper
> and special sense of the divine vocation which is direct-
> ed to the lay faithful. They are not called to abandon
> the position that they have in the world. . . . On the
> contrary, he entrusts a vocation to them that properly
> concerns their situation in the world. The lay faithful,
> in fact, "are called by God so that they, led by the spirit
> of the Gospel, might contribute to the sanctification of
> the world, as from within like leaven, by fulfilling their
> own particular duties."[9]

The common priesthood and the ordained priesthood are distinct
in nature but united by their shared call to sanctification. This leads
us to the pivotal chapter of *Lumen Gentium*, "The Universal Call
to Holiness in the Church."

Summoned to Sainthood

Chapter 5 of *Lumen Gentium* is groundbreaking. Not since the
apostolic age has such a compelling explanation of the People of
God's baptismal call been accessible. For the majority of Church
history, sainthood was seen as a calling reserved for clergy and
religious. For a clear indicator of how widespread this notion has
been, just look at the number of canonized laypeople compared to
saints who are ordained or religious. This is to say nothing against
the saints or the Church's canonization process. It makes sense that
those who are consecrated live extraordinarily holy lives and have
renowned influence on the universal Church. That being said, the
council wanted to reclaim the idea, present from the time of the
apostles, that baptism in and of itself is a summons to sainthood.
"Thus, it is evident to everyone, that all the faithful of Christ of
whatever rank or status, are called to the fullness of the Christian
life and to the perfection of charity" (*LG* 40).

St. Josemaría Escrivá anticipated the upcoming teachings of
Vatican II when he founded Opus Dei in 1928: "It is in the midst

of the most material things of the earth that we must sanctify ourselves, serving God and all mankind."[10] Lay movements were popping up throughout Europe and America in the years preceding the council. It was clear that the Holy Spirit desired a renewal of baptismal identity among the faithful.

The Spirit's rationale makes sense amidst our current socio-economic situation. Globalization coupled with an ever-increasing secularism presents a new set of challenges for the cause of evangelization. Like never before, clergy, religious, and laity need to make a collaborative and organized effort to ensure that the Gospel is preached to the next generation. Only when the whole Church is united in the pursuit of holiness can it be truly effective in ministering to the world. In many ways, our generation of Catholics is reminiscent of the ancient Church—persecuted, mocked, suppressed, and silenced. We will need to lean on each other in the years to come, encouraging one another in Christ so as to continue our task of sanctification.

This was the collaboration Satan sought to destroy with the clergy sex-abuse crisis. The horror of these scandals has left a deep wound in the hearts of both clergy and laity. If Satan can sever the intimate relationship between the faithful and their pastors, then neither will receive what they need from the other. A shepherd who is at arm's length from his flock is ineffective and lonely. A flock that feels distant from its shepherd is disheartened and lukewarm. Bridging the gap and rebuilding the trust between the lay faithful and clergy is vital to our mission. We cannot allow the evil of some to suggest that none are holy. Priests cannot let fear and anxiety keep them from building relationships with families and children. Of course, this must always be done with prudence and obedience to the regulations given by our bishops. Nonetheless, it is so desperately needed—the People of God are aching for it. Laypersons should pray constantly for priests, deacons, and religious, begging God to keep them safe and restore a sense of joy in their hearts.

"The forms and tasks of life are many, but holiness is one—that sanctity which is cultivated by all who are moved by the Spirit of God, and who obey the voice of the Father and worship God the Father in spirit and in truth" (*LG* 41). We are all called to be saints. Every man, woman, and child, wherever they find themselves, are given the vocation of holiness. We do not become saints outside of our reality. Holiness is not to be found anywhere else but right in front of us. Our families, spouses, children, professions, schools, grocery stores, law firms, Twitch, YouTube, sporting events—these are the people and places we are called to make holy and convert to Christ. If every Catholic lived with this mentality, society would be transformed. I am a missionary, and wherever I stand is my mission ground. Whatever situation I find myself in, that is where Jesus wants me to become a saint.

Few better exemplify this way of life than St. Thérèse of Lisieux, the Little Flower. She longed to be numbered among the great saints of Church history but knew she could not possibly accomplish the extraordinary things they did in their lives. Thérèse was dispirited, thinking that there was no place for someone like her in the Church. She felt so little and insignificant. Then, in a moment of prayer, the Lord taught her a great mystery for which Thérèse became not only a saint, but a Doctor of the Church:

> When I had looked upon the mystical body of the Church, I recognized myself in none of the members which St. Paul described, and what is more, I desired to distinguish myself more favorably within the whole body. Love appeared to me to be the hinge for my vocation. Indeed, I knew that the Church had a body composed of various members, but in this body the necessary and more noble member was not lacking; I knew that the Church had a heart and that such a heart appeared to be aflame with love.... Then, nearly ecstatic with the supreme joy in my soul, I proclaimed: O Jesus, my love, at last I have found my calling: my call is love.

> Certainly, I have found my place in the Church, and
> you gave me that very place, my God. In the heart of
> the Church, my mother, I will be love, and thus I will
> be all things, as my desire finds its direction.[11]

St. Thérèse found her place in the Church. It was a little place, seemingly inconsequential and ineffective in the eyes of the world. But, in the eyes of God, it was the greatest of vocations. The same is true for each of us. There is a place for you in the Church, a calling that God has given you that no one else can replace or fulfill. You are called to become a saint; don't miss the opportunity.

We Are a Pilgrim People

One final component of being the People of God is appreciating the fact that we are a pilgrim Church, a people on the way. The Church is a sacrament. Thus, she points to something in our midst as well as something beyond us—to what is, but also to what is to be. In describing the Church as a pilgrim people, the Second Vatican Council reintroduces a concept from the ancient Church, namely, the eschatological nature of the Church. The word "eschatological" refers to the Second Coming of Jesus. Although Christ's salvation has been realized in the Church, we are still on a journey. Until the Lord comes again, "some of His disciples are pilgrims on earth [the Church militant], some having died are purified [the Church penitent in purgatory], and others are in glory beholding 'clearly God Himself triune and one, as He is' [the Church triumphant in heaven]" (*LG* 49).

The council indicates the eschatological nature of the Church as a pilgrim people by noting that she exists in the simultaneous tension of "already" and "not yet" (*LG* 48). The victory of Christ is already here—Christ has died and risen. But it is also not yet—Christ will come again. One of the Eucharistic prefaces in the Roman Missal says it this way: "Now, as your Church makes her pilgrim journey in the world, you always accompany her by the power of the Holy Spirit and lead her along the paths of time to the eternal joy of your Kingdom."[12] Until that time, we remain to adore Christ in the world with our eyes fixed on the heavenly Jerusalem.

The Blessed Virgin Mary

Along with ecclesiology, Mariology—the study of the Blessed Virgin Mary—likewise experienced a revitalization in the nineteenth and twentieth centuries due largely to the impact of patristics. Whereas Möhler and Newman championed the cause of ecclesiology, the study of Mariology found its champion in the person of Fr. Matthias Joseph Scheeben (1835–1888). A German theologian and mystic, Scheeben is one of the main theologians responsible for the renewal of Marian studies. Scheeben's writings on Our Lady are some of the most moving and beautiful texts in recent Church history. He seamlessly weaves the wisdom of the Church Fathers into the fabric of his own scholarship. Although the pre-conciliar Church thrived in devotion to the Blessed Mother, the patristic connection between Mary and the Church was muted. Scheeben was among the first to gather these ancient teachings and crystallize them within the mainstream theology of the Church.

The influence of the Church Fathers' Mariology led to two major, infallible declarations in the decades before Vatican II: the Immaculate Conception, declared by Pope Pius IX in 1854, and the Assumption of the Blessed Virgin Mary, declared by Pope Pius XII in 1950. Both of these pronouncements were bolstered by the two great Marian apparitions of the nineteenth and twentieth centuries: Our Lady of Lourdes in 1858 and Our Lady of Fatima in 1917. It was clear that the Blessed Mother needed to have an active and appreciated role in the Church of the twentieth century.

Vatican II's intent to dedicate a document to Our Lady became a point of contention in the council. Some wanted the Blessed Mother to have her own document, while others thought the writing on Mary should be coupled with the constitution on the

Church, *Lumen Gentium*. After fierce debate, the council voted to include the section on Mary with the document on the Church, making it the closing section.

At first glance, this may seem like an insignificant detail. But theologically it makes a big difference. By placing the section on Mary within the document on the Church, Vatican II is making a claim about the role of Mary in the life of the Church. She is not someone separated from the Church, nor is she a person of interest outside of the Church. Rather, her existence is intrinsically bound to the life of the Church as the Bride of Christ and Mother of Nations. To appreciate the full depths of this reality, we need to reflect on Mary's essential role throughout the major events of Christ's life.

Since the close of Vatican II, there has been an egregious decline in Marian devotion throughout the wider Church. This is especially true in the United States. No doubt, the influence of Protestantism is partially to blame—even though the reality is that the hypercritical attitude toward Mary is a relatively recent development in Protestantism. The first Protestants were not anti-Marian. King Henry VIII had a strong devotion to the Blessed Mother even as he founded the Church of England. Ulrich Zwingli, John Calvin, and Thomas Cranmer, all of whom were involved in founding distinct strands of Protestantism, vehemently maintained Mary's role in salvation history. Among the Protestant founders, none was more passionate about their love for the Blessed Virgin Mary than Martin Luther himself, who wrote several works promoting devotion to the Mother of God. Most astonishing of these is a work in which *he defends the Immaculate Conception of Mary*, a Catholic doctrine that would not be officially recognized until three hundred years after his death!

It is for this reason that I often say jestingly that the first task of Catholics is not to convert Protestants to Catholicism but to convert Protestants to Protestantism. But I mention these things merely to tear the mask off of the accusation that Marian devotion is something foreign to Christianity. The question is not, "Should we honor the Blessed Virgin Mary?" but rather, "How should we honor the Blessed Virgin Mary?"

Another factor in the decline of Marian devotion is the lack of catechesis among the faithful regarding Mary. Most laypeople see Mary as important simply because she birthed Christ, after which she is basically irrelevant to salvation. Few appreciate Mary's active role in salvation after the Nativity, and it is rarely preached in homilies or spoken about in parish missions. *Lumen Gentium* spends a considerable chunk of its eighth and final chapter discussing the role of the Blessed Mother in the plan of salvation:

> The Sacred Scriptures of both the Old and the New Testament, as well as ancient Tradition show the role of the Mother of the Savior in the economy of salvation in an ever clearer light and draw attention to it. . . . The earliest documents, as they are read in the Church and are understood in the light of a further and full revelation, bring the figure of the woman, Mother of the Redeemer, into a gradually clearer light. . . . She stands out among the poor and humble of the Lord, who confidently hope for and receive salvation from Him. With her the exalted Daughter of Sion, and after a long expectation of the promise, the times are fulfilled and the new Economy established, when the Son of God took a human nature from her, that He might in the mysteries of His flesh free man from sin. (*LG* 55)

As we dive more deeply into the life of this woman through sacred scripture, the writings of the Church Fathers, and chapter 8 of *Lumen Gentium*, I pray we will come to a deeper appreciation of her role in the life of the Church and the invaluable vocation she possesses as mother of all Christians.

The Blessed Virgin Mary in Salvation History and the Life of the Church

Let us begin our reflections on the Blessed Mother with the first words spoken to her in sacred scripture. We read in chapter 1 of Luke's gospel that the angel Gabriel was sent to Nazareth to a virgin named Mary. When he arrives, he greets the young maiden with the following words: "Hail, favored one!" (Lk 1:28). There are several topics to be considered from this single phrase. First, we must appreciate the speaker. The person saying these words is not some random guy. It is an angel! The word "angel" comes from the Greek word *ággelos*, which means "messenger."

In ancient times, the *ággelos* of a king or aristocrat was received as the personal embodiment of the individual they represented. They did not come to speak their own opinion; they were expressly sharing the thoughts and feelings of their master. The words of Gabriel are not his words, then, but God's words. The angel is simply a messenger of what he has been told to speak. When Gabriel says to Mary, "Hail!" (*Χαῖρε*), a salutation of profound honor reserved for royalty, it is God saying these words. Thus, we find the source and origin of Marian veneration is God himself. Catholics did not invent honoring the Blessed Virgin Mary—God did. We simply seek to be obedient to the Lord's example of reverence for her.

Another fascinating linguistic point: The conjugation of the Greek word used in Luke 1:28 is employed only four other times in the New Testament. Each use is associated with Christ's Passion, specifically when the guards are mocking Jesus' kingship, saying "Hail (*Χαῖρε*), King of the Jews!" (Mt 27:29; Mk 15:18; Jn 19:3). This is a beautiful theological connection. From the moment the angel Gabriel meets Mary of Nazareth, her life is intricately bound to the Passion and Death of her beloved son. The full ramifications of this connection will not come to light until the Crucifixion.

The next vital part of the angel's greeting is his designation of Mary as the "favored one." This English translation fails to capture the full signficance of the original Greek. St. Jerome more accurately translated the phrase as "gratia plena," meaning "full of grace." But what does "full of grace" mean? The Greek word for "full of grace" is *kecharitōmenē* (try saying that ten times fast). Its literal translation is, "you who have been made to be graced." Yes, this is who Mary truly is—the one whom God created to be graced, the pure tabernacle he created to bear the greatest treasure of all, his only-begotten Son.

In the Gospel of Luke, 1:39–45, we read about the Visitation of the Virgin Mary to her cousin Elizabeth. On hearing the voice of the Blessed Mother, the infant in Elizabeth's womb leapt for joy and the aging woman, "filled with the holy Spirit," exclaimed, "Most blessed are you among women, and blessed is the fruit of your womb" (Lk 1:41–42). This interaction between Mary and Elizabeth is so rich in theological content and historical significance that it will be impossible to adequately address all of the details within this book. But let us seek at least to scratch the surface of this highly momentous biblical event.

There are five persons immediately involved in the Visitation. On the one hand, we have Elizabeth and John the Baptist. Elizabeth is the wife of Zechariah, a priest of Israel. John, their son, is the one destined to be the final prophet of the Jewish nation. Thus, we see in the persons of Elizabeth and John the Baptist an embodiment of the Old Testament in its priestly and prophetic role. On the other hand, we have the Virgin Mary and Jesus Christ. The womb of Mary is the new ark of the covenant holding a treasure much greater than the rod of Jesse or the tablets of God's commandments (see Hebrews 9:4). Rather, within her is held the incarnate fulfillment of the Law and the prophets. It is for this reason that St. Luke mentions John the Baptist "leaping" in the womb before the Blessed Mother. Just as King David danced before the ark of the covenant when it was brought into the city of Jerusalem (see 2 Samuel 6:14), so now John the Baptist dances before the new ark of the covenant as she ushers in him who is the hope of all peoples.

The Church Fathers marveled at this connection between the ark of the covenant and the womb of Mary. St. John of Damascus preaches about it with rousing prose in his homily *On the Nativity of the Holy Theotokos*:

> Let the celebrated tabernacle which Moses construct-
> ed in a desert with all manner of very precious metals
> . . . give way to the living and rational tabernacle of
> God. . . . Let a tabernacle that was entirely covered with
> gold recognize that it cannot compare with her, along
> with a golden jar that contained manna, a lampstand, a
> table, and all the other objects from long ago. For they
> have been honored as her types, as shadows of a true
> archetype.[13]

The Visitation is the personified meeting of the Old Testament and the New Testament. In the embrace of these two mothers and their sons, we witness the people of the Old Testament embracing the Church of Christ. This meeting is mediated by the fifth person present at the visitation, the Holy Spirit, who himself declares Mary's fidelity and preciousness to God when he inspires Elizabeth to praise the Virgin's faith: "Blessed are you who believed" (Lk 1:45). Yes. Blessed is she whose faith is greater than that of Abraham or Jacob, Moses or Isaiah, Esther or Deborah. Blessed is she who believed and whose faith opened the way for Christ's coming into the world.

Immediately following Elizabeth's declaration of Mary's blessedness among women, the Virgin bursts into a song of joy, praising God for his faithfulness and mercy. This hymn of praise is one of the most beautiful prayers in the history of Christianity. In fact, the words of Our Lady in Luke 1:46–55 have become a fundamental devotion in the piety of the Church, repeated by millions of Christians throughout the centuries as an inspiring summary of the soul's sense of gratitude before the grandeur of God's love: "My soul proclaims the greatness of the Lord" (Lk 1:46).

The Greek word used for "proclaims" is *megalunó,* a verb coming from the prime root *megas,* which means "to magnify [in the sense of a magnifying glass], extol, or enlarge." Thus, within the first line of this canticle we see revealed an essential characteristic of the Blessed Virgin Mary: Hers is the heart that "magnifies," brings into complete focus, humanity's response to the salvation God desires to share with the world in the person of Jesus Christ. After all, was it not from her lips that the human race finally said yes to God's will? The whole world awaited Mary's reply in Nazareth; all of creation held its breath, longing for the Virgin's acceptance of her destiny. St. Bernard of Clairvaux captures this sentiment well in a sermon he addressed to Our Lady:

> In your [Mary's] brief response we are to be remade in order to be recalled to life. . . . This is what the whole earth waits for prostrate at your feet. It is right in doing so, for on your word depends comfort for the wretched, ransom for the captive, freedom for the condemned, indeed, salvation for all the sons of Adam, the whole of your race.[14]

Mary knows what the acceptance of God's will means for her: "From now on will all ages call me blessed" (Lk 1:48). She does not say these words out of pride, but rather from a place of humility and astonishment. "For he [God] has looked upon his handmaid's lowliness. . . . The Mighty One has done great things for me, and holy is his name" (Lk 1:48–49). Mary truthfully recognizes the level of dignity to which God has raised her. Her desire is simply to love him and see him adored, yet, for a reason beyond her understanding, *he has chosen* to exalt her alongside her son. *He has chosen her* to be the personal embodiment of "daughter Zion" (Zep 3:14), and now, through her trusting confidence in his will, he will help

"Israel his servant . . . according to his promise to our fathers, to Abraham and to his descendants" (Lk 1:54–55). How could anyone possibly question the honor given to the Blessed Virgin Mary by God himself? How can we call ourselves Christians if we refuse to acknowledge the special role God has chosen for this woman whom all generations call blessed?

The incarnation of God in the person of Jesus Christ is the perfect union of heaven and earth. The divine is wedded to the human. This union begins in the womb of the Blessed Virgin Mary, the new ark of the covenant, when she conceives the Son of God. For nine months this great treasure remains hidden in the body of Our Lady, a joy that only she can truly understand. Then, in the city of Bethlehem, under the shadow of a cave turned into a makeshift stable, the child she has nourished and protected is given to the world: The creature gives birth to her Creator. The historical and symbolic significance of this event cannot be overstated, particularly in regard to the relationship between Christ and his mother.

From the beginning the Church has recognized the correlation between the events of Jesus' birth and death; his infancy and Passion go hand in hand. The first thing Jesus touches in his life will be the last thing he touches in his life: wood. In the wood of the manger we see a prelude to the wood of the Cross. Likewise, the ancient artists of the Church deliberately depict the child Jesus as if prepared for burial, covered in a white cloth from head to toe. Here we see a link between the "swaddling clothes" (Lk 2:7) with which Jesus is wrapped on the day of his birth and the "linen cloth" with which he is wrapped on the day of his death (Lk 23:53). There is much more that could be said about the allusions strewn throughout the infancy narrative predicting the Passion. But these two examples are sufficient to highlight our point, namely, that the Blessed Virgin Mary was the only person present at both of these decisive events in salvation history.

At the birth of Jesus, which must be interpreted in light of his death on the Cross, we find Mary the faithful stewardess, kneeling in silent and tender adoration. As she cradles and gazes on the face of her child—the only child in history who was born to die—her pride of place in the story of salvation is clearly revealed. Hers are the arms by which God's longing to be held by humanity is satisfied, just as hers are the arms that will embrace the crippled, tortured body of her beloved son after he has satisfied man's desire to be held by God. Thus, in the Nativity, we find Our Lady at the intersection of two infinite thirsts: God's thirst for humanity and humanity's thirst for God.

We see a similar dual significance of Mary in the two interactions between Jesus and his mother recorded in the Gospel of John: the Wedding Feast at Cana (John 2:1–12) and the conversation on Golgotha (John 19:26–27). These interactions between Our Lady and Jesus are rich in spiritual content. We have to remember that John's gospel is the latest of the four gospels, composed sometime around the year AD 90. As such, it contains a highly matured theological perspective on Christ's person and mission, and represents the deeply mystical reflections of a developed Christian paradigm. The reader will recognize very quickly that the two interactions described by John, one ushering in the ministry of Christ and the other consummating that same ministry, are intricately intertwined.

Jesus' first miracle is performed at a wedding. This is no small detail. By drawing our attention to this important fact, John gives us the lens by which to interpret the entirety of Jesus' mission. As we have mentioned before, Christ is the new Adam who has come to be wedded to his people, Israel. Yet, the new Adam needs a new Eve: This is the infrastructure of creation and salvation. By assuming the sex of a male, Jesus places himself in a posture that necessarily demands the cooperation of another. Not just any other, but that other who is the man's "helper," namely, Eve (Gn 2:18). It is for this reason that Mary is present at this crucial moment in Christ's life.

Furthermore, her presence is not coincidental. Rather, Mary plays a vital role in the prompting of Jesus' miraculous action. Where the first Eve failed to call Adam to greatness, the new Eve succeeds by drawing out of the new Adam a manifestation of his glory. This is the constant task of Our Lady—to be that guiding principle who opens the eyes of humanity to the glory of her son. When Mary tells the servers at the wedding feast, "Do whatever he tells you" (Jn 2:5), her words encapsulate her entire vocation. Every word and action of her life point toward her son. Her heart is so entirely Christian (from the Greek word *christianoi*, meaning "belonging to Christ") that it can only lead us to Jesus.

We turn now to the interaction between Christ and his mother on Calvary. One of the fundamental flaws of contemporary Christianity is a reduction of the Blessed Mother and her role in the process of salvation. She is seen by some Christian denominations as nothing more than a temporary vessel, a sort of divine petri dish used by God to self-cultivate his own humanity and so enter the physical realm.

Yet, the original Christian tradition (that is, Catholicism) has always seen Mary's significance in its entirety. The Annunciation and Nativity of Christ are properly understood as only the beginning of Mary's mission. In truth, the fullness of Mary's role in salvation history is revealed at the foot of the Cross. At that moment, from the bloodied lips of our tortured Savior, we hear a stunning declaration addressed to Mary and St. John the Apostle: "Woman, behold your son" (Jn 19:26). These are not simply the words of a temporary adoption or some form of ancient social security program. Christ is making an official decree as to the role of the Blessed Mother in Christianity.

There are two points of interest in this passage. First, Mary is addressed *before John*. This is no coincidence. As with all things in the life of Christ, this too is by design. Mary is spoken to first because she is the primary recipient of the gift of Christ crucified. She is the prophesied "daughter Zion" (Is 62:11; Mi 4:13; Zec 9:9) who receives the gift of the crucified God indefectibly and definitively on behalf of Israel and indeed all of creation. She is the creature of God par excellence, uncorrupted and thus able to unconditionally and freely accept the sacrificial love of her son. Her yes to Christ's sacrifice is what makes our yes possible. For, if Mary had not been present at the Crucifixion to witness and accept the sacrifice of her son, which is the ultimate gift of the Father to humanity, then no other human person could share in the fruit of its salvation.

This sheds light on the second point of the passage. Mary is addressed as "woman." The Lord recognizes the Blessed Virgin at this moment as more than just his biological mother; she is woman, *the* woman above all other women. Just as Adam, when looking at the creature God had formed out of his side in the Garden of Eden, called her "woman" (Gn 2:23), so now, the new Adam looks down on the creature who will be created out of his pierced side, the new Eve, and calls her "woman" (Jn 19:26). From her devotion is born the identity of the Church as *Sponsa Christi*, "Spouse of Christ." Thus, Mary is not merely a member of the Church—she *is* the Church in person and as person. This is why since the beginning, the Church has been referred to in the feminine. The Church is not an "it" but a "she," because at her core lies a specific personality—and that person is Mary.

"Behold, your mother," Jesus says to John (Jn 19:27). John, the beloved disciple, is given to Mary as a son, and Mary is given to the beloved disciple as a mother. What is the significance of this adoption? Up to that moment, the heart of Mary had been crushed and broken as she watched her son being murdered. Now, the reason behind such affliction is made plain. The crushing of the mother's heart has been for the sake of its renovation and expansion—a reforging of her motherhood to embrace the entirety of God's children as represented in the person of John.

Now she, the Immaculate One who assented wholehearted-ly to God's mission, will become the model and patroness of all those who strive to love her son. At last, the vocation of Our Lady is fully revealed. She is not simply Jesus' biological mother. Her role in Christianity is much more radical. Given to each other as a gift, the mother and the disciple must love one another. From the Cross, Christ makes clear the fact that a relationship with his mother is not an option for his disciples; she was essential for his life and so it will be for all of those who desire to follow him. In this declaration, Christ expands the heart of his mother to enfold all of the faithful.

Devotion to Mary—to know her and to love her—is therefore not some cultic invention of medieval Catholicism; *it is a basic Christian attitude*. Intrinsically tied to witnessing her son's death and receiving the Father's will for him on the Cross, Mary's virginal heart—which provided a home for God—now provides a home for all humanity. Now she is not only *Sponsa Christi*, but *Mater Ecclesia*, "Mother Church."

Hans Urs von Balthasar points out that Christ placing Mary into the care of John permanently inserts her into the life of the Church. "In so doing, He gives the Church her center or apex: an inimitable, yet ever-to-be-striven-for embodiment of the new community's faith, a spotless, unrestricted Yes to the whole of God's plan for the salvation of the world."[15]

This is a vital component of our understanding of the nature of Mary and the Church according to Vatican II: "As St. Ambrose taught, the Mother of God is a type of the Church in the order of faith, charity and perfect union with Christ. . . . The Church indeed, contemplating her hidden sanctity, imitating her charity and faithfully fulfilling the Father's will, by receiving the word of God in faith becomes herself a mother" (*LG* 63). The motherhood of the Church flows from the motherhood of the Blessed Virgin. And everything the Church does is first realized in the life of Mary.

This truth is expressed wonderfully in the Eucharistic preface for the Roman Missal's Mass dedicated to Mary, Fountain of Light and Life:

> By the marvelous gift of your loving kindness
>   you decreed that the mysteries
>   accomplished already in the Blessed Virgin
>   should be accomplished in sign
>   through the sacraments of the Church:
>   for from the Baptismal font the Church brings to birth
>   new sons and daughters conceived in fruitful virginity
>   through faith and the Holy Spirit.
> Each day the Church also prepares for its children
>   the table where it nourishes them with the Bread of
>   Heaven,
>   born of the Virgin Mary for the life of the world:
> Jesus Christ the Lord.[16]

Mary's role as Spouse of Christ and Mother Church are not exclusive to her relationship with God, but represent all of us who are baptized. With this in mind, we can properly appreciate the necessity of the dogmas of the Immaculate Conception and the Assumption. Mary is immaculate not just for the sake of bearing Christ in her womb, *but also for the sake of becoming the Church.* Furthermore, she is united body and soul in heaven with God, thus realizing the reality of the Church as a pilgrim people living in the "already, but not yet" of salvation. Finally, she is an eschatological sign—a focal point on which we can constantly gaze as a reminder of what we all will become if we model ourselves on her faithfulness.

This is why the Church is incorruptible, indefectible, and immaculate no matter the sins or scandals of its members. She is and always will be the spotless bride, "without spot or wrinkle or any such thing . . . holy and blameless" (Eph 5:27). I do not say this to overspiritualize or downplay the sins of the Church. On the contrary! I am placing the Church's sins in perspective. Like a light fixed in the dark, the humble faithfulness of our Blessed Mother pierces through the sins of every clergyman and layperson. The promise made by Christ to preserve the Church from corruption remains valid, and no one from the pope to the parochial vicar can invalidate it. For there is one who is faithful, even when I am not, and her name is Mary, Mother Church. The closing words of *Lumen Gentium*'s chapter on the Blessed Virgin Mary provide a fitting ending for this chapter:

> The entire body of the faithful pours forth instant supplications to the Mother of God and Mother of men that she, who aided the beginnings of the Church by her prayers, may now, exalted as she is above all the angels and saints, intercede before her Son in the fellowship of all the saints, until all families of people, whether they are honored with the title of Christian or whether they still do not know the Saviour, may be happily gathered together in peace and harmony into one people of God, for the glory of the Most Holy and Undivided Trinity. (*LG* 69)

5

DIVINE REVELATION

The Second Vatican Council's Dogmatic Constitution on Divine Revelation, *Dei Verbum*, is the shortest of the four major council documents. The topic of divine revelation was initially introduced in 1870 during the First Vatican Council in its Dogmatic Constitution on the Catholic Faith (*Dei Filius*). Yet, there needed to be a deeper reflection on the essence and sources of divine revelation. Thus, the original draft of the Vatican II document was entitled *De fontibus revelationis*, "On the Sources of Revelation." Divine revelation was a topic of vehement debate during the council and one of the more divisive subjects among the bishops. At question was the relationship between tradition and sacred scripture, as well as the historicity and inerrancy of the Bible—which is to say, whether what the Bible teaches is without error and completely true.

The conversation was necessary because of advances in biblical scholarship throughout the nineteenth and twentieth centuries. A lot had changed since the Council of Trent's decrees on the Bible in 1546. Both Catholic and Protestant Bible scholars were making strides in the field of scripture study. In particular, use of the historical-critical method was gaining great acclaim and many adherents. The historical-critical method takes a particular approach to the study of scripture, focusing especially on three elements to draw out the meaning of a word, verse, or passage: historical context, intent of the author, and the designated audience of the author. The historical-critical method is especially useful for gaining a better understanding of the development, authorship, and reception of sacred scripture—but the method is not without its dangers. We will discuss the council's opinion on the historical-critical method and its role in interpreting scripture later in the chapter.

But first, we need to begin with the topic of divine revelation itself. What is divine revelation, and how is it transmitted to us? Chapters 1 and 2 of *Dei Verbum* address these questions. Then we will talk about the proper interpretation of sacred scripture and the role of sacred scripture in the life of the Church.

What Is Divine Revelation?

What is the Word of God? Most people would say that the Bible is the Word of God. Yet, that is not what the Bible says: "In the beginning was the Word, and the Word was with God, and the Word was God . . . and the Word became flesh and made his dwelling among us" (Jn 1:1, 14). The Word of God is not a book, but a person, Jesus Christ. This understanding has been present in Catholicism since the beginning. St. Gregory of Nazianzus says, "From the Father is the great God's Word: eternal Son, the archetype's image, a natural equal to His parent."[1] St. Augustine likewise exhorts the congregation listening to his homily on John 1:1 that Christ is "the God-Word with God, through whom all things were made; for that is life which in Him is the light of men."[2]

To appreciate the ancient Church's teachings on Jesus as the Word of God, we must look at the original Greek. The Greek noun translated "Word" in our Bibles is *logos*. It is the origin of the English word "logic." When St. John proclaims Christ as the Word of God, he is stating that Christ is the incarnate logic of God. When the second person of the Trinity becomes flesh, he reveals the deepest essence of the Father's heart. "Whoever has seen me has seen the Father" (Jn 14:9), and "No one comes to the Father except through me" (Jn 14:6). Christ is the logic of God; he reveals how God exists, acts, thinks, and feels. St. Maximus the Confessor reiterates this point when he says, "The Logos [Christ], by essence God . . . when He became man . . . established Himself as the innermost depth of the Father's goodness."[3]

The Second Vatican Council, in perfect continuity with tradition, asserts that "in His goodness and wisdom God chose to reveal Himself and to make known to us the hidden purpose of His will by which through Christ, the Word made flesh, man might in the Holy Spirit have access to the Father and come to share in the divine nature" (*DV* 2). Divine revelation is God's unveiling of himself throughout history. This unveiling reached its pinnacle in Jesus Christ. He is the fullness of divine revelation, "the center of the universe and of history."[4] Everything in the Old Testament tended toward Christ, and everything in the New Testament flows from him. Jesus is the Word spoken by the Father in whom all the secrets of the Godhead are laid bare. It is Christ crucified who reveals the depths of God's heart as his own heart is torn open with a lance. Now, nothing of God is held back; he gives himself completely to the world in the person of his Son. "For God so loved the world that he gave his only Son" (Jn 3:16).

This means that sacred scripture does not reveal God's mysteries in and of itself; rather, it is a testament of the One who is the Word. Thus, the ancient Church drew a distinction between the Word of God and sacred scripture. As Hans Urs von Balthasar says, "Scripture is not the Word itself, but rather the Spirit's testimony concerning the Word which springs from an indissoluble bond between the Spirit and those eyewitnesses who were originally invited and admitted to the vision."[5]

After the Protestant Reformation, the distinction between the written word of the Bible and Jesus as the eternal Word of God began to get muddled in certain circles, in part because of the Protestant teaching of *sola scriptura*, "scripture alone." The sacramental focus of Christianity diminished in favor of a "personal relationship" with Jesus based on reading the Bible and the private assimilation of faith. Slowly but surely, the theology of the Word-made-flesh gave way to a theology of the word of scripture and "Bible-based" communities.

The Catholic Church, on the other hand, is not a Bible-based Church in the Protestant sense. Rather, we are rooted in the living presence of Jesus in the sacramental life of the Church. We are not a religion of the book alone, but a faith of the Christ who is in our midst. We are living stones built upon the chief cornerstone (see 1 Peter 2:5–7). We do not encounter Christ as pure spirit or abstract concept. Christianity is not something you read about. It is someone you meet in the flesh in a truly personal way through the sacraments. "Look at my hands and my feet, that it is I myself. Touch me and see, because a ghost does not have flesh and bones, as you can see I have" (Lk 24:39). The resurrected Christ is one who must be touched and embraced—body, blood, soul, and divinity.

This emphasis on Christ as the Word of God in the fullest sense does not degrade the dignity of the Bible or make it irrelevant in any way. On the contrary, it places the Bible in context, allowing us to engage the text as a medium of encounter with the living Word. "For ignorance of scripture is ignorance of Christ."[6]

There is a desperate need within the Church to reclaim the distinction between the Word of God and sacred scripture in the hearts of the faithful. If not, our theology of the Word will remain shallow. We will lose the vitality of the Word while scripture becomes a self-help book, a set of rules, or inspirational literature in the spirit of Joel Osteen or Joyce Meyer. Theologians and priests have the responsibility of making the distinction in homilies, parish talks, and theological writings. We must also be careful in our language. I hear many people describe the Bible as the Word of God without making the explicit connection to Christ as the living Word. Although this is not heretical in any way, it does lack a certain intellectual subtlety that can lead to misconceptions about the Church's theology.

Thankfully, there are several recent thinkers who have made great strides in recultivating a theology of the Word. On the Catholic side, Balthasar helped to reclaim this way of thinking in *The Word Made Flesh* (the first volume of his *Explorations in Theology*) as well as in *The Glory of the Lord*. On the Protestant end, Karl Barth reinvigorated such theology in both *Church Dogmatics* and *The Word of God and Theology*.

We have discussed how Vatican II preaches Jesus Christ as the fullness of divine revelation. He is the Word of God who dwells among us and in whom we see the face of the Father. Now, let us reflect on how this truth is transmitted throughout history.

Sacred Tradition and Sacred Scripture

"In His gracious goodness, God has seen to it that what He had revealed for the salvation of all nations would abide perpetually in its full integrity and be handed on to all generations" (*DV* 7). We do not follow Christ secondhand. In order to follow him, we have to meet him and know him. That is why St. Paul is adamant about the centrality of the Resurrection for Catholic faith: "If Christ has not been raised, your faith is vain" (1 Cor 15:17). If Christ himself is the fullness of divine revelation, if he is the foundation of Christianity, then he needs to be alive. We cannot love a memory; we can only love a person. Jesus must be alive, or else Christianity is dead. Thus, Jesus assures his apostles that he is "not a ghost" in his post-Resurrection appearances, even going so far as to take the hand of Thomas and thrust it into his own pierced side (see John 20:27). It is necessary, therefore, that Christ provide a means of self-communication after his Resurrection and Ascension. He must hand on his ministry. He does so through sacred tradition and sacred scripture.

Tradition comes from the Latin *traditio*, meaning "to hand over." Jesus founded an infrastructure through which his presence could be mediated. We see this at the Last Supper. During these final moments of his earthly life, Jesus established a ritual to both continue his act of worship of the Father (the Eucharist) and minister to his people (the priesthood). When he met the apostles in the upper room after the Resurrection, he breathed on them and gave them the authority to bind and loose sins (see John 20:23–24). Later, he tasked them with spreading the Gospel through the *sacraments* ("Go, therefore, and make disciples of all nations, baptizing them" [Mt 28:19]) and *preaching* ("teaching them to observe all that I have commanded you" [Mt 28:20]). "This commission was faithfully fulfilled by the Apostles who, by their oral preaching, by example, and by observances handed on what they had received from the lips of Christ" (*DV* 7).

The divine revelation of Christ entrusted to the apostles in the sacraments and preaching is preserved in sacred tradition and sacred scripture. This is properly called the deposit of faith. These two realities together serve as the Church's source of wisdom and holiness as she seeks to do God's will in the world. "This sacred tradition, therefore, and Sacred Scripture of both the Old and New Testaments are like a mirror in which the pilgrim Church on earth looks at God, from whom she has received everything, until she is brought finally to see Him as He is, face to face" (*DV* 7).

An essential component of sacred tradition is something called apostolic succession. "In order that the full and living Gospel might always be preserved in the Church, the Apostles left bishops as their successors giving them their own position of teaching and authority" (*DV* 7). Because of apostolic succession, there is an unbroken connection between the Church of the past and the Church of today. We are inheritors of a tradition "built upon the foundation of the apostles and prophets, with Christ Jesus himself as the capstone" (Eph 2:20). "The Tradition that comes from the

Apostles makes progress in the Church, with the help of the Holy Spirit" (*DV* 8).

Tradition is not stagnant, but progresses in history. The Church is living and so is constantly being purified and renewed (*LG* 8). She is also continually growing in a deeper understanding of salvation. The mystery of Christ is inexhaustible. Every day we learn something from him and find another reason to love him. That is the whole reason behind synods and councils. They are gatherings that allow us to reflect on salvation and better appreciate it. Then, with renewed gratitude, we seek to share our joy through evangelization. A synod or council is primarily for the betterment and sanctification of its participants. It is an occasion for contemplation and prayer, allowing Christ to reinvigorate souls and guide the Church's ministry.

"By means of the same Tradition the full canon of sacred books is known to the Church and the holy Scriptures themselves are more thoroughly understood and constantly actualized in the Church" (*DV* 8). The Bible is the testament of tradition, which is to say, the document of the Church's encounter with Christ as inspired by the Holy Spirit. According to Vatican II, the fullness of Christ's truth can only be experienced in the cooperation of sacred tradition and sacred scripture. Alone, neither of these realities is sufficient. The Church does not draw all her certainties about the faith from the Bible alone, nor does she disregard the scriptures in favor of tradition. "Therefore, both sacred tradition and Sacred Scripture are to be accepted and venerated with the same sense of loyalty and reverence" (*DV* 9).

The body of bishops entrusted with protecting tradition, faithfully interpreting sacred scripture, and governing the Church is called the magisterium. The magisterium possesses authority over the Church in the name of Christ. After Vatican II, the authority of the magisterium was regarded with suspicion by some paraconciliar theologians. Hans Küng, for example, in his book *The Catholic*

Church: A Short History was keen on depicting the hierarchy of the Church as a political body conniving and pulling strings for its own good.

Yet, the problem lies in a misunderstanding of the true meaning of "authority."

The word "authority" shares a root with the Latin *augmentum*, which carries the idea of "causing to grow." Originally, it was an agricultural term referring to the tilling of fields. That shared root reveals a nuance that's significant for our understanding of ecclesial authority. While power is involved in any notion of authority, the Church's power is meant to be directed toward care and nourishment. Those who have authority are tasked with fostering the growth of others. They are caretakers of people's hearts. The magisterium has been assigned the responsibility of fostering growth in holiness among the People of God. This can only be accomplished if the magisterium is faithful to the deposit of faith. Sacred tradition is the field of souls, the space in which they take root through the sacraments. Sacred scripture is the fertilizer. Through the preaching of pastors and catechesis, the field is tilled for harvest.

Interpreting Sacred Scripture

At the beginning of this chapter we gave a brief background of the history of interpreting scripture in the twentieth century. Among the main topics of discussion in Vatican II was the role of certain contemporary methods in the study of sacred scripture, most notably, the historical-critical method. What are the pros and cons of the historical-critical method, and how can it be properly integrated into the Church's study of scripture?

First, the cons. When the historical-critical method is used in isolation, it reduces sacred scripture to a purely worldly thing, void of any mystical or spiritual depth. An exclusive commitment to the historical-critical method shrinks sacred scripture to a mere collection of proverbs, life lessons, narratives, and mythological stories. Anything that appears to be supernatural is dismissed as fantasy, interesting only insofar as it reveals something about the religious ideas and mindsets of ancient cultures. Biblicists of this sort demote miracles and salvation events to a subset of religious literary tropes within the raw data of the scripture texts. In short, the historical-critical method treats scripture as a relic of the past as opposed to a dynamic word that is "living and effective" (Heb 4:12). This is why Balthasar warned those who use the historical-critical method in interpreting the Bible to not act like a coroner dissecting a corpse: "For, we can be sure of one thing, we can never recapture the living totality of form once it has been dissected and sawed into pieces, no matter how informative the conclusions which this anatomy may bring to light."[7]

The exclusive use of the historical-critical method for interpreting scripture is prevalent in paraconciliar thought. Some clergy and theologians claim that events such as the feeding of the five thousand were not miracles but sociological phenomena.[8] According to this view, Jesus did not actually multiply food from the fishes and loaves; rather, his words and example inspired the people to share the food they had brought among themselves. The true "miracle," therefore, was that Jesus moved the crowd's hearts from selfishness to generosity. This represents a shallow and untheological reading of the text. It also discounts the Church's long-standing tradition of interpreting this event as a precursor to the Eucharist and a symbol of Christ nourishing the nations with his own Body and Blood.

The misuse of the historical-critical method deprives the faithful of the full wealth of scripture. A homilist may explain the historical aspects of scripture, but it is to no avail if he cannot place the readings within the context of Christian tradition. It is valuable, for example, to discuss the practices of first-century Judaism and their relation to Jesus' comments on the Sabbath. But it remains stale data if we do not take the next step by mentioning how the Church Fathers interpreted these comments as an allusion to the

Resurrection and the role of the Sabbath in Christian life. Thus, when Jesus said that "the sabbath was made for man, not man for the sabbath" (Mk 2:27), he was not only criticizing the hypocrisy of the Pharisees and correcting Jewish Sabbath laws; he was also providing the spiritual foundations for a true understanding of his Resurrection and its relation to the Sabbath. The Sabbath is for man because *Christ is for man*; he comes to saves us. The fruits of the Sabbath signified in the laws of Torah are fulfilled completely in the Resurrection of Christ, who establishes a new Sabbath sourced in communion with the Church. Going to Mass on Sundays, therefore, is indispensable to Christian living because it is the place where Christ is *for* you and where we experience communion with the God who loves us.

Reacting to the paracouncil's misappropriation of the historical-critical method, some traditionalists reject it wholesale. They denounce it as a secular tool that disregards the dignity of sacred scripture. This too is incorrect. If used properly, the historical-critical method is an asset to the spirituality of sacred scripture. A good example is the story of the hemorrhaging woman in the Gospel of Luke. This woman had suffered bleeding for twelve years. But when she touched Jesus, she was instantly healed of her illness. At face value, this is already a moving story of faith and healing. But the historical-critical method reveals certain subtleties that help us appreciate the real profundity of this encounter.

According to the purity laws of Judaism, a woman with a flow of blood is considered unclean. This woman was effectively excluded from the common life of her village and disconnected from the liturgical worship of Israel. Her willingness to be seen by a crowd of people exhibits great faith and courage as those who were aware of her condition would have most certainly looked down on her.[9] Another striking detail is that under those same purity laws, any man touched by a bleeding woman is considered unclean. This sheds light on why the woman attempted to touch Jesus secretly, grasping furtively at the hem of his cloak. Jesus was a holy man of reputation, and the woman did not want to shame him. So, she "came up behind him and touched the tassel on his cloak. Immediately her bleeding stopped" (Lk 8:44).

Jesus could have continued walking, keeping the miracle quiet. Instead, he turns and asks, "Who touched me?" (Lk 8:45). It is Jesus who makes this healing a public affair. Regardless of the shame he will likely incur, Christ desires to bring this woman out of the shadows. She who lived on the margins of society as an outcast is now held up in the sight of all as a model of Christian faith: "Daughter, your faith has saved you" (Lk 8:48). Daughter! How powerful that designation is, especially when we understand the full social and cultural context! When was the last time anyone had called this woman "daughter," intentionally and publicly associating himself with her? Everyone she knew was ashamed of her, embarrassed to be in her presence. She had lived in obscurity for over a decade, but now this man called her daughter.

This, then, is an example of how the prudent application of the historical-critical method can enrich our study of sacred scripture. The broader context reveals how great the divine mercy of Jesus is. Not only does he take us out of the shadow of sin and remind us of our dignity as children of God, but he does so with no regard for his own reputation. He is not embarrassed to be our friend, our brother, our Savior.

We have taken this homiletical detour to illustrate the reality that science is not opposed to faith and scholarship is not an enemy of spirituality. The key is making sure that one is subject to the other: The historical-critical method is good, but it is not the highest good. It cannot be used profitably in isolation from tradition and faith.

So what does a Catholic interpretation of sacred scripture look like in light of *Dei Verbum*'s teachings? Pope emeritus Benedict XVI provides the beginnings of an answer in his *Jesus of Nazareth*

series. Noting the tension that exists between a spiritual interpretation of scripture and the historical-critical method, Pope Benedict
proposes a collaboration between the two. He states that a properly
informed faith hermeneutic can be combined with a historical
hermeneutic to produce a more Catholic understanding of sacred
scripture.[10] Vatican II says something similar in paragraph 12 of
Dei Verbum:

> Since God speaks in Sacred Scripture through men in
> human fashion, the interpreter of Sacred Scripture, in
> order to see clearly what God wanted to communicate
> to us, should carefully investigate what meaning the
> sacred writers really intended, and what God wanted
> to manifest by means of their words. . . . But, since
> Holy Scripture must be read and interpreted in the
> sacred spirit in which it was written, no less serious
> attention must be given to the content and unity of the
> whole of Scripture if the meaning of the sacred texts
> is to be correctly worked out. The living tradition of
> the whole Church must be taken into account along
> with the harmony which exists between elements of
> the faith. (*DV* 12)

The council encourages the use of contemporary methods of scholarship in scripture study, as long as they are kept in perspective. The
Bible is the Church's book. It can only be fully understood within
the Body of Christ. By itself, its wisdom remains only partial. But
in cooperation with tradition, the full brilliance of scripture is
revealed. This is why Vatican II strongly "encourages the study
of the holy Fathers of both East and West and of sacred liturgies"
(*DV* 23). Ongoing engagement with the writings and teachings of
the Church Fathers is vital to the renewal of the Church and the
work of biblical scholarship.

The Church is still navigating the waters of Bible scholarship
according to Vatican II. In fact, we are in need of theologians and

Bible scholars who produce holistic interpretations of sacred scripture using contemporary methods of scholarship while weaving the
fruit of their study into the wider tradition of the Church, especially
the writings of the Church Fathers. Unfortunately, as Pope Benedict points out, this has scarcely been attempted thus far.[11] There
are some examples that inspire hope, such as John Bergsma and
Brant Pitre's outstanding commentary, *A Catholic Introduction to
the Bible*. But overall, there remains a gap in the field of biblical
studies between sound theology and exegetical research.

A vital step, therefore, in reclaiming Vatican II's legacy for
the Church today must be the training of a generation of faithful,
liturgically formed men and women as Bible scholars. They must
be firmly rooted in the theology and traditions of the Church, while
also proficient in the very best methods and insights on offer from
modern biblical scholarship. Vatican II charts a path for just this
kind of bold, fruitful engagement.

6

THE CHURCH AND THE MODERN WORLD

The last of the four major documents of Vatican II is the Pastoral Constitution on the Church in the Modern World, *Gaudium et Spes*. Yet again, the ordering and flow of the documents reveal the working of divine providence. As we noted in chapter 2, there is a fundamental logic to the council. The life of the Church is sourced in the sacred liturgy. It is from the work of the liturgy that the Church's essential nature shines forth. This Church is nourished and guided by divine revelation, as given to us in sacred scripture and sacred tradition. Now the council focuses on the natural consequence of the liturgy and divine revelation: evangelization. *Gaudium et Spes* stands apart from the other major council documents as a *pastoral* constitution rather than a *dogmatic* constitution. In other words, its primary concern is not a particular doctrine of the Church, but the care of souls. It is intended to guide the Church in her mission of evangelization and salvation.

This makes perfect sense when you consider that one of the chief architects of *Gaudium et Spes* was Cardinal Karol Wojtyła, now known as St. John Paul II. The saint's fingerprints are all over the document. It reads like one of his encyclicals and focuses on many of the same themes: the dignity of the human person, the sanctity of marriage, the right to property.

Gaudium et Spes is the longest of the four major council documents and discusses a wide variety of topics. There are numerous books that go into detail about the anthropology and socioeconomic decrees of *Gaudium et Spes*. We will only mention these things in passing as they are already a topic of regular reflection in the Church. However, there are certain key teachings of the document that relate to our aim of reclaiming Vatican II. Specifically, we will focus on the council's teaching on the Sacrament of Marriage, which is a landmark work in Church history. First, a few notes about the document's background.

Overall, *Gaudium et Spes* represents a true shift in the Church's posture toward the world. Before Vatican II, the Church's general attitude toward secular society was isolationist and critical. There were multiple reasons for this, and not all of them were bad. The Church's defenses had been on high alert since the Protestant Reformation. From that point forward, it had seemed as if everything was falling apart, as if the whole infrastructure of Christendom was under attack. The next several centuries of Catholicism were rocked by one revolution after another. In a series of shifts initiated during the Enlightenment and catalyzed by the Industrial Revolution, Western civilization was drifting from its Christian roots. Add to that the tragedy of two world wars, socialist uprisings, and a rapidly growing global economy—and you have the recipe for turbulent times. The Church had to discern her place in a world that was becoming increasingly antagonistic, and it was not immediately clear how to address the needs of the time. Secularism, atheism, agnosticism, rationalism, scientism, communism, socialism, and every other ism you could imagine were vying for the souls of God's people.

The council fathers knew that circling the wagons was no longer viable. It was time for a radical change in technique. Thankfully, the Lord raised several brilliant theologians and clergymen to aid in the task. Karol Wojtyła, Joseph Ratzinger, Henri de Lubac, Yves Congar, Karl Rahner, and many others worked tirelessly to provide a theological basis for reform. Likewise, the Holy Spirit was inspiring the formation of numerous ecclesial movements throughout Europe and America in the years immediately preceding Vatican II. Organizations such as Communion and Liberation in Italy and the Catholic Worker Movement in the United States were indicators of the hunger in people's hearts for the Church to be active in an ever-changing world.

Gaudium et Spes represents the Church's never-ending quest to evangelize culture. That quest demands a keen awareness of the problems that face humanity at any given historical moment. The most impressive thing about *Gaudium et Spes* is its ability to "judge the signs of the times" (Mt 16:3). Any accusation that the Catholic Church is out of touch or ignorant of the world is debunked within the first few paragraphs of *Gaudium et Spes*. In reality, the Church is an expert in humanity. She knows the "joys and the hopes, the griefs and the anxieties of the men of this age, especially those who are poor or in any way afflicted" because "these are the joys and hopes, the griefs and anxieties of the followers of Christ. Indeed, nothing genuinely human fails to raise an echo in their hearts" (*GS* 1). The Church is not a spectator in the world. When society suffers, so does the Church. She is bound to her people as a mother is to her children. Vatican II recognizes the suffering of so many in the modern world. It also recognizes that the Church has the truth the world needs to hear if this suffering is to be redeemed.

Jesus Christ: The Center of Civilization

Gaudium et Spes begins by asking a basic question: What is the situation of humanity in the world today? With striking clarity, the council answers, "Man is growing in awareness that the forces he has unleashed are in his own hands and that it is up to him to control them or be enslaved by them. Here lies the modern dilemma" (*GS* 9). The world is in a state of flux and often runs before it can walk. We are progressing so rapidly in the fields of technology, science, and economics that we are not able to keep up even with ourselves. There is a sense of constantly being overwhelmed by the world we have created. So much is happening so fast. Pope Benedict XVI summarizes the phenomenon well:

> Less visible, but not for that reason less disturbing, are the possibilities of self-manipulation that man has acquired. He has investigated the farthest recesses of his being, he has deciphered the component of the human being, and now he is able, so to speak, to "construct" man on his own. This means that man enters the world, no longer as a gift of the Creator, but as the product of our activity. . . . In this way, the splendor of the fact that he [man] is the image of God—the source of his dignity and of his inviolability—no longer shines upon this man; his only splendor is the power of human capabilities. Man is nothing more now than the image of man.[1]

Pope Benedict's statement highlights an important paradigm shift that has taken place in the modern world. Before the sixteenth and seventeenth centuries, Western civilization possessed a basically Christian outlook on the world, which is to say, it understood reality through the assumption of a distinction between a transcendent Creator and all the created order. According to this view, all of reality comes from and is rooted in God the Creator. He creates *ex nihilo*, "out of nothing." Everything God creates is unnecessary to his being, yet he creates it anyway. Thus, creation is most fundamentally a gift given by God. Creation is an act of love. This being the case, all of creation is infused with value and worth loving: the sky, the birds, our fellow humans. Likewise, all of creation is good since it comes from God and is willed by him. This is especially true of humanity, which is made in God's likeness and image and willed for its own sake. Every human being is created by God for the purpose of dwelling in communion with him.

Modernity flips this notion on its head. There is no God—or if there is, it is simply one thing among others in the universe. The world is an accident sourced in a mathematical probability and decipherable through scientific calculation. Humanity is the animal lucky enough to be able to decode these equations and manipulate matter through knowledge and technology. Things are not "created" in the sense of being willed for a higher good, but are coincidental, the products of causation and natural selection. "This alters the basic relation of man to reality. He now views reality essentially from the functional point of view."[2]

From this perspective, a thing's value is not measured in terms of its own goodness, but by its usefulness for a variety of arbitrary goals. If something cannot produce favorable results, it can be discarded. This logic, in its most extreme forms, applies even to people—which is why something like euthanasia makes sense in the modern world. The person in a coma no longer has "quality of life." They can no longer produce anything or live as they would like to. Thus, their life is worthless. They are broken, a dysfunctional cog in the machine. Plus, they are a drain on the economy and a source of pain for their loved ones. Eliminating them will solve all of those problems.

This chilling logic is prevalent in our society. And though a complete diagnosis goes beyond the purview of this book, we can at least say that its rise is partially traceable to scientific and technological capabilities that have advanced without an accompanying moral maturity. The human being is composed of body and soul. Everything we do has a spiritual effect, whether we believe it or not. The modern world prioritizes bodily satisfaction, but ignores spiritual development—predictably resulting in internal conflict and anxiety. "The dichotomy affecting the modern world is, in fact, a symptom of the deeper dichotomy that is in man himself" (*GS* 10). Our bodies are comfortable, but our souls are starving, and this imbalance causes strife. The vast majority of people in the world are not attending to their spiritual needs. They run about chasing every whim, fad, and pleasure, but arrive home empty every night. What an exhausting way to live! The dissatisfying cycle is enough to make one question whether life has meaning.

One of the greatest threats in the modern world is atheism. The council dedicates a significant portion of chapter 1 of *Gaudium et Spes* to detailing the reasons for and effects of atheism. And it identifies the core danger of atheism: its contradiction of the very nature and ultimate end of the human person, namely, to be in full communion with God. Yet, in a refreshing change of tone, the council provides an incredibly pastoral response to atheism. It does not condemn atheists, nor does it belittle their reasons for their beliefs. Rather, the council seeks to affirm the good that atheism is trying to find. For Mother Church tries "to seek out the secret motives which lead the atheistic mind to deny God. Well knowing how important are the problems raised by atheism, and urged by her love for all men, she considers that these motives deserve an earnest and more thorough scrutiny" (*GS* 21). The Church wants to enter into an active dialogue with atheism, knowing that a world without God is a world where humanity is lost and miserable. *Gaudium et Spes* makes it clear that the Church does not desire such a fate for any person.

To respond to the existential crises of the modern world, *Gaudium et Spes* offers an insightful reflection on the dignity of the human person in light of Jesus Christ. At the center of this reflection is a paragraph that has become synonymous with *Gaudium et Spes* and indeed captures the key teaching of the document:

> The truth is that only in the mystery of the incarnate
> Word does the mystery of man take on light. For Adam,

> the first man, was a figure of Him Who was to come,
> namely Christ the Lord. Christ, the final Adam, by the
> revelation of the mystery of the Father and His love,
> fully reveals man to man himself and makes his supreme
> calling clear. (*GS* 22)

Jesus Christ reveals man to man. What a profound statement! Whereas atheistic society seeks to find the meaning of life in scientific achievement and political power (often gained through violence), the Church holds up Jesus Christ and his humanity as our model and guide. Jesus Christ came to give us life—abundant life (Jn 10:10). He is the truth made flesh, and in him we find our destiny. All the aspirations and ideals of humanity are realized in Jesus Christ. His light and life must be the center of civilization.

This paragraph in *Gaudium et Spes* displays the theological depth of the council's thinking. Traditionalists dismiss the council as being shallow and worldly in its theology. They are particularly critical of *Gaudium et Spes*, supposing that it is little more than a piece on social justice. But paragraph 22 exhibits the contrary. *Gaudium et Spes* is not merely a social justice manifesto. Nor does it pander to secular society. It is a document centered on Jesus Christ, as is every document of Vatican II. Paragraph 22 is the interpretive key for understanding the entirety of *Gaudium et Spes*. The document's teachings on human community, social justice, marriage, and the economy all flow from it.

The Preservation of a Humane Culture and Social Justice

Chapter 1 of *Gaudium et Spes* focuses on the universal vocation of humanity to holiness and communion with God. Chapter 2 expands this concept in relation to human community and culture. If the purpose of human life is to be with God, then culture must revolve around this goal and provide an environment for it to be achieved. This can only be accomplished if the Church actively engages with the world, reminding men and women of their lofty vocation as pilgrims on a journey to the heavenly city (*GS* 57). Thus God desires that all human persons "should form one family and deal with each other in a spirit of brotherhood" (*GS* 24). This necessitates building a society of love and justice—which requires a foundation of respect for the inherent dignity of the human person. The council proves itself prophetic in its writings on human life. The council fathers' awareness of the challenges and threats to human life is stunning as is their ability to clearly identify the consequences of such threats:

> Coming down to practical and particularly urgent consequences, this council lays stress on reverence for man; everyone must consider his every neighbor without exception as another self, taking into account first of all his life and the means necessary to living it with dignity, so as not to imitate the rich man who had no concern for the poor man Lazarus. . . . Furthermore, whatever is opposed to life itself, such as any type of murder, genocide, abortion, euthanasia or willful self-destruction, whatever violates the integrity of the human person. (*GS* 27)

Vatican II is clear in asserting the dignity of human life and specific in identifying the practices that assault that dignity. This prophetic call remains a crucial task for the Church today. Society has gotten worse since Vatican II on issues related to respect for human life and sexual morality. If the council fathers were to rewrite the document today, no doubt they would include in vitro fertilization, embryonic stem-cell research, pornography, gay marriage, and transgenderism on the list of threats to human dignity. The Church has a complex and redeeming theology of life and sexual morality. But it is rarely discussed or taught to the faithful in its full context.

Chapter 2 also introduces the Church's dialogue on social justice. In recent years, social justice has become a central focus of the

Church. My seminary professor once said that Catholic social justice doctrine is one of the Church's best-kept secrets, meaning that the theology and teachings of the Church's social justice doctrine remain widely unknown. This is due in part to the paracouncil's use of *Gaudium et Spes* as a means to support specific political ideologies and social programs. In some instances, such as that involving the revolutionist priest Fr. Ernesto Cardenal, members of the Church even resorted to violence in the name of social justice. Treating the Church's teachings on social justice as a call to revolution—or using them to support non-Catholic political or economic ideologies such as communism—is to lose sight of their spiritual core.

Vatican II's true teaching on social justice, rather than defining a series of specific rules or applications, is primarily spiritual in nature, focusing on the conversion of human hearts so as to affect the infrastructures of society. There must be an internal conversion if we are to make external changes. Thus, the section on social justice is preceded by a paragraph on respect and love for enemies: "Respect and love ought to be extended also to those who think or act differently than we do in social, political and even religious matters. In fact, the more deeply we come to understand their ways of thinking through such courtesy and love, the more easily will we be able to enter into dialogue with them" (*GS* 28).

This instruction remains as relevant as ever, if not more so. As our culture has become increasingly polarized, many of us have forgotten how to dialogue with one another. We have forgotten the art of disagreement. In times past, foes in a philosophical debate could still be friends in the pew. People on the other side of the political aisle could sit at the same table for dinner. But now, we seem unable to distinguish between an individual's ideas and their inherent dignity as a person. *If your ideas are bad, then you must be bad too. If I hate your politics, that means I hate you.* Too many of us have lost the ability to make intellectual distinctions and temper our emotions with reason. Utilizing the teachings of *Gaudium et Spes*, the Church can aid in the rehabilitation of civility, love, and hope in our culture. Although true justice begins in the human heart, it is not meant to be confined there. The Church does have a say in working concretely and practically toward an equal and prosperous society for all peoples. We are called to evangelize the world.

To this end, chapter 4 of *Gaudium et Spes* reflects on the relationship between the Church and the world. It is once again worth mentioning the humble and pastoral tone of the document. Vatican II writes about not only what the Church offers the world, but also what the world offers the Church: "Just as it is in the world's interest to acknowledge the Church as an historical reality, and to recognize her good influence, so the Church herself knows how richly she has profited by the history and development of humanity" (*GS* 40).

These words of the council teach us a valuable lesson. If we want to work with someone, we need to be willing to affirm the good that they are seeking. This is a basic Catholic principle of dialogue. It is impossible for someone to truly desire evil for the sake of evil. Rather, everyone desires a good even if they are going about it in the wrong way. The philosophies and ideals of the modern world can teach us a lot about the state of the human heart in our time and the goods people desire.

Few better characterized the ideal of compassionate dialogue than St. John Paul II. The holy pontiff tirelessly preached the culture of life and civility in both word and action. Whether it was his historic 1979 homily behind the iron curtain of Communist Poland or his merciful embrace of the man who shot him in St. Peter's Square, St. John Paul II embodied the Catholic principle of dialogue with culture—one that recognizes the common humanity of all people and the Gospel's role in ensuring that same humanity's cultivation. Coupling the rich intellectual tradition of Catholicism with an infectious, joyful piety, St. John Paul II shows us that *Gaudium et Spes*'s teachings are indispensable to society.

In a time when so many people are searching for a wise and courageous voice, the Church is called to enact her God-given genius, building bridges of fraternity and fostering a civilization of love. This begins with our own personal witness to the joy (*gaudium*) and hope (*spes*) of Catholicism. There is nothing in the world more beautiful than the Catholic Church. She is the spotless bride of Christ (see Ephesians 5:27), the perfect fruit of the Son's sacrifice. As such, the Church is meant to be a school of culture, an exemplar of what the world should be, and the sacrament of what God accomplishes in the hearts of those who trust in him.

Thus, the Church maintains an indispensable role in the world. She is not simply one institution among others. Her vocation is unique and essential to civilization. The "Church, at once a visible association and a spiritual community, goes forward together with humanity and experiences the same earthly lot which the world does. She serves as a leaven and as a kind of soul for human society as it is to be renewed in Christ and transformed into God's family" (*GS* 40). The Church is the spiritual mentor of culture. In some ways, we have surrendered culture to secular powers. Yet, the Church is the best culture builder. We know that from history. Christ is the foundation of true culture. His life is what renews human culture when it is plagued by egoism and superficiality. Meeting Christ opens new horizons in our hearts and allows us to cultivate culture more deeply.

Vatican II on Marriage and the Family

No council in history dedicated more effort and time to the laity than Vatican II. In addition to expounding on the lay state of life, the council fathers also provide a powerful reflection on the vocation of marriage as a sacrament and its foundational role in establishing and maintaining a healthy society. Vatican II's decrees on marriage and the family are magnificent and represent the clearest articulation of the sacrament in Church history. Anyone who is discerning marriage, in marriage formation, or already married should read *Gaudium et Spes*, part II, chapter 1. I require all of the couples I am preparing for marriage to read it. It will also prove beneficial to priests and formators of married couples.

Right out of the gate, the council fathers make a bold claim about marriage: "The well-being of the individual person and of human and Christian society is intimately linked with the healthy condition of that community produced by marriage and family" (*GS* 47). Without healthy marriages, society is not healthy. In the United States, 39 percent of all marriages end in divorce.[3] In 2018 alone, more than 780,000 people got a divorce or annulment. These statistics are indicative of the moral and societal health of our country. Thousands of children are being raised without a mother or father, and many more are brought up in abusive homes. There are many dangers to marriage and family life. So-called free love, pornography, homosexual lifestyles, transgenderism, substance abuse, and financial strain all pose threats to the stability of marital union. "Furthermore, married love is all too often dishonored by selfishness, hedonism, and unlawful contraception" (*GS* 47). All of these problems reveal grave misunderstandings about sexuality, gender, and love.

Too many of our kids learn about sexuality from Google and the porn industry. In our public school system, Planned Parenthood is the single largest sex education provider in the United States, offering classes on sexuality to more than 1.5 million children from elementary to high school every year. These classes include education on the use of contraception and abortion, which are presented as normal health practices. In the 2019–2020 television season, over 10 percent of all the fictional characters portrayed on broadcast television were LGBTQ.[4] In the area of cultural norms for marriage, family, and sexuality, the entertainment industry is mounting a full-court press for the hearts and minds of today's youth—and it is winning. I am sad to say that even in some of our Catholic schools, I have seen rainbow flags and banners promoting the gay agenda and ideologies that run counter to the Church's clear teachings. We need to reclaim Vatican II's teachings on the dignity of human life and the related questions of sexual morality.

There are some who shy away from discussing human life and sexual morality issues. It is an uncomfortable subject for both clergy and parents. But the fact that we are not talking about it openly and honestly is having serious consequences. Priests in particular need to form their hearts according to the teachings of the Church so as to give parents resources to help their children. "It devolves on priests duly trained about family matters to nurture the vocation of spouses by a variety of pastoral means, by preaching God's word, by liturgical worship, and by other spiritual aids to conjugal and family life; to sustain them sympathetically and patiently in difficulties, and to make them courageous through love, so that families which are truly illustrious can be formed" (*GS* 52).

The paracouncil caused its own set of problems for marriage and family life after Vatican II. This began with the outright rejection of St. Paul VI's encyclical on human life, *Humanae Vitae*. Numerous clergy in the 1960s, '70s, and '80s taught that contraception and self-sterilization were acceptable in Catholic doctrine. I have spoken with several people who got sterilized at the suggestion of their priest, who told them they had "fulfilled their duty" of having children after two kids. Vatican II, according to these priests aligned with the paracouncil, did not require such couples to remain open to life. That was old pre–Vatican II teaching, they said. In some cases, gay marriage was openly supported by priests and preached from the pulpit. Men and women were told in the confessional that looking at pornography is not a mortal sin. Young people confused about their gender were encouraged to explore their identity and discover who they really were.

The paracouncil's sexual ethics left its mark on a whole generation of Catholics and their children. It also hollowed out the profundity of the Church's marriage theology. Even now, Catholic teachings on sexuality and marriage remain basically undiscussed at the average parish. I believe this is due to an insecurity about sexuality in general, which has been heightened by the clergy sex-abuse scandal. Thankfully, the Second Vatican Council provides a sophisticated dissertation on sexuality, marriage, and the family rooted in sacred scripture. Let us spend some time reflecting on it.

In the Gospel of Matthew we read that some Pharisees approached Jesus and tested him, asking, "Is it lawful for a man to divorce his wife for any cause whatever?" (19:3). The Lord responded, "Have you not read that from the beginning the Creator 'made them male and female'?" (19:4). Instead of getting caught up in the details of Judaic marital law, Christ draws the listener into a deeper meditation on the overall mystery of marriage by alluding to the Book of Genesis and God's original intent for creation. St. John Paul II reminds us that by referencing "the beginning," Jesus alludes to God's original plan for creation.[5] So doing, the Lord provides a key for the authentic understanding of matrimony.

In the first creation account, we hear God say, "Let us make human beings in our image, after our likeness" (Gn 1:26). Note God's use of the first-person plural when referring to himself—the ancient Church recognized this as a direct reference to the Blessed Trinity. If God is a communion of persons united in love, and humanity is made in his image, then humanity shares (in a creaturely manner) in the divine qualities of communion and love. This fact distinguishes Adam from the other creatures in the Garden of Eden. Unlike plants, which are bound by natural law, or animals, which are driven by basic instinct, Adam possesses an acute awareness that he is different. Thus, none of the creatures in the garden prove to be a "a helper suited to the man" (Gn 2:20).

St. John Paul II in his famous theology of the body calls this phenomenon "original solitude." According to the pope, Adam— who is a representation of all humanity—is a unique being in the created world. As a creature gifted with intellect, he must find his purpose for living. He experiences a deep need to understand who he is and why he exists. "Thus, the created man finds himself from the first moment of his existence before God in search of his own being . . . one could say, in search of his own definition; today one would say, in search of his own 'identity.'"[6] In so doing, Adam realizes his innate longing for an "other," one who is like himself with whom he can share communion. He desires to be a gift. God responds by creating woman, at which Adam cries out in thanksgiving, "This one, at last, is bone of my bones and flesh of my flesh" (Gn 2:23).

Here we see the initial plan for marriage. Man and woman are made in the likeness of the Trinity. Thus, their sexual and spiritual union is an icon of the union that exists between the Father, Son, and Holy Spirit. This union is intended for fruitfulness: "By their very nature, the institution of matrimony itself and conjugal love are ordained for the procreation and education of children, and find in them their ultimate crown" (GS 48).

The early Church, following the precedent set by Matthew 19, used Genesis as its starting point in the consideration of Christian marriage, yet with an added dimension. After the Crucifixion, Resurrection, and Ascension of Christ, the apostles' eyes were opened to the overarching plan of God's saving work in history. For, "in times past, God spoke in partial and various ways to our ancestors through the prophets; in these last days, he spoke to us through a son" (Heb 1:1–2). This newfound paradigm made it possible to see the Old Testament as a protoevangelium, a prophetic precursor to the Gospel, a preparation for the Church. This led in turn to the development of a rich theology—particularly in regard to the Sacrament of Marriage.

St. Paul's letter to the Ephesians represents the height of Christian marriage theology:

> Husbands, love your wives, even as Christ loved the church and handed himself over for her. . . . "For this reason, a man shall leave his father and his mother and be joined to his wife, and the two shall become one flesh." This is a great mystery, but I speak in reference to Christ and the church. (Eph 5:25, 31–32)

The apostle reminds us that Christian marriage is a sacrament of Christ's love for the Church. Every activity of a Christian husband and wife—their heart-filled embrace, their parting kiss, their joint gaze upon a newborn child—reflects the love of Christ for the Church. This is how marriage is a sacrament. As such, the love shared between a husband and wife is not merely their own but is also "caught up into divine love and is governed and enriched by Christ's redeeming power and the saving activity of the Church" (*GS* 48). The contemporary crisis of marriage is a direct result of forgetting these truths about matrimony. Marriage simply cannot be understood apart from its sacramental character. Attempts to extract marriage from its sacramental meaning will result in a pale counterfeit, a mere contract. But a deep understanding of marriage in all its rich sacramental character can make it a source of inspiration and renewal in the world.

At this point, it is worth interjecting a brief commentary on the council's teaching about procreation and contraception. As noted earlier, the paracouncil promoted teachings against Vatican II in these areas. As a result, many Catholics believe the same things about sexuality and reproduction as any secular person. One of the biggest tragedies of modern times is the widespread use of contraception. Vatican II explicitly condemns this practice:

> From the moment of its conception life must be guarded with the greatest care while abortion and infanticide are

> unspeakable crimes. The sexual characteristics of man and the human faculty of reproduction wonderfully exceed the dispositions of lower forms of life. Hence the acts themselves which are proper to conjugal love and which are exercised in accord with genuine human dignity must be honored with great reverence. . . . Relying on these principles, sons of the Church may not undertake methods of birth control which are found blameworthy by the teaching authority of the Church in its unfolding of the divine law. (*GS* 51)

When sex becomes an end in and of itself—artificially severed from its natural goal of procreation—then human life becomes a dispensable option. The dignity of the person becomes secondary to his or her immediate desires. St. Paul VI warns about the dangers of such a mentality in *Humanae Vitae*.[7] When human life is optional and dependent on individual interests, then all bets are off. If we can't even be open to the possibility of life, how can we be expected to respect it in all its other stages? Children are always a gift, and Catholics are morally obligated to uphold the right to life and promote a culture that supports families.

This leads us to the final part of *Gaudium et Spes*'s writings on marriage. The family is the nucleus of civilization. "Thus, the family, in which the various generations come together and help one another grow wiser and harmonize personal rights with the other requirements of social life, is the foundation of society" (*GS* 52). If we want to heal society, Vatican II tells us, begin with healing families. The Church should be the first in line to foster healthy family life. So many families nowadays feel as if they are flying solo. This is especially true for young Catholic families. They want to have a holy marriage and raise their children right, but have no one to turn to for guidance and encouragement, even in the Church.

A young mother once came to my office in tears after encountering some older women in the parish. They were talking about their families, and she mentioned that she wanted to have several more children. The older women scoffed at the idea and said, "Why would you want to do that? You already have three kids. You should get fixed and forget about it." What disturbed the young lady the most was not so much the comments, but the fact that they came from practicing Catholics who she thought would support her love for life.

The walls of our parishes need to be a refuge for families, a place where they can go to feel safe and supported. I had the privilege of growing up in a poor mission parish in Central Florida. It was established to serve the Puerto Rican population who worked in the hotels and theme parks of Orlando. I can say without exaggeration that St. Catherine of Siena was my second home. I *lived* at that church. All of my childhood friends were children from the parish. The doors were always unlocked, and the church was constantly filled with young families and children. Our pastor was very welcoming to the families. He always made a special effort to make mothers and fathers with crying babies feel comfortable during Mass. A baby once started crying during his homily. When the father of the child stood up and tried to remove the baby as quickly as possible from the room, the priest said, "Please, sir, that child is part of our family. It is okay if he cries. That means that our parish is alive."

If the Church ain't cryin', then it's dyin'. I am personally opposed to cry rooms in churches—they send a bad message. If we truly value life and marriage and children, how can we dare to communicate, "All are welcome in this place . . . unless you are a parent with a screaming child"? Mothers and fathers should not feel embarrassed or anxious about bringing their children to Mass. I publicly thank young families in my parish during the Sunday Mass on a regular basis. I want them to know that we recognize their sacrifice. I also want them to feel appreciated. Not too many twenty- and thirty-year-olds are getting married anymore, and it is likely that many of those who do marry are not going to Mass every Sunday. Having young families going to Mass is a blessing, and we should let them know it. A child should grow up seeing the parish as their second home. The only four walls the child should know better than their church are the four walls of their house.

Priests and families are meant to collaborate in raising holy families. The couples should be able to look to the priest for spiritual leadership, virtuous living, Christian friendship, and wise advice. Children should see the priest as an example of holiness, a trusted confessor, and a joy-filled disciple of Jesus. Yet again, this is an area where the abuse crisis has devastated the Church. That essential relationship between priests and families has been shattered. Suspicion, anxiety, and shame have replaced trust, peace, and freedom. Some priests won't even hug a child for fear of being misperceived or falsely accused. I thank God that he has allowed me to have close friendships with several families. I have known some of them for many years. Recently, one of the dads told me that his teenage son gets more excited when Fr. Blake comes over for dinner than when his friends do. This is how it should be. The priest is an integral member of family life. He is a figure that should be associated with families and their constant resource for joy and inspiration.

Steps to Foster Vatican II's Teachings on Marriage

We do have some viable tools in place to help us tap into Vatican II's tremendous resources for invigorating and healing our understanding of the Sacrament of Marriage and its many interconnections with family life and sexual morality.

Christian Education: An Indispensable Foundation

We must start with a renewed emphasis on the spiritual formation of our children in families, Catholic schools, and faith-formation programs. Marriage prep should start in childhood. It is in the context of the home and the parish community that a person first learns how to love, sacrifice, forgive, and pray—all attributes necessary for a healthy marriage. A more theological explanation of marriage would be helpful for middle school and high school students. St. John Paul II's theology of the body is a valuable resource. The Theology of the Body Institute provides wonderful study programs for teens and young adults. Priests, religious, and laypeople also need to be properly formed in the area of sexuality and Christian anthropology. Those who receive appropriate training can then return to their faith communities and begin establishing programs for the education of parents and children.

Marriage Preparation: A Process of Formation

To be ordained a priest, I was required to spend nine years in serious discernment aided by spiritual direction, formation advisement, and an evaluation process. Yet, some couples make a lifelong commitment to their spouse and God after only a few marriage-prep sessions and a retreat weekend! To me, this seems grossly unbalanced, especially considering the gravity of the marriage sacrament. I am not saying that there necessarily needs to be a longer time period of marriage prep. But I do believe that marriage-prep programs need a serious overhaul. This should include more spiritual and catechetical formation of couples. Integrating the reading of Vatican II documents, papal encyclicals, and patristic sources will also prove invaluable to the couple and their understanding of Christian marriage.

As with Christian education, the preparation of married couples needs to be seen as a formation process that shapes the mind, heart, and soul. Whether both of the spouses are Catholic or only one, the dignity and sanctity of the bond remain. The formation should correlate with this reality. Once again, the theology of the body would be of great service. Letting couples know the power and beauty of their conjugal love is absolutely crucial to strengthening their self-gift while properly disposing them to be open to life and family.

Accompaniment of Families: Making Their Vocation a Priority

Finally, priests and lay leaders must make it a pastoral priority to accompany families. This can happen by having parish groups that are dedicated to family life. At our parish we started a family life ministry. Families meet on the first Friday of every month for their "Family First Friday" Eucharistic Holy Hour followed by a potluck dinner. Occasionally, we invite a guest speaker for dinner to give catechesis on a variety of topics. Spiritual direction and Confession are also offered for the parents and children. The benefits of this ministry are truly incredible. It creates a sense of community and a sort of "school of the family" that is seriously lacking in our society. Furthermore, the parents are more dedicated than ever to the parish because they see the Church making their vocation a priority. Even our parish school enrollment has gone up because of this ministry. Healthy families, holy parishes.

7

WHAT NOW?

The Second Vatican Council was the most important event in the Catholic Church of the twentieth century. Yet, its teachings remain shrouded behind a veil of unfamiliarity, and its vision continues to be widely misrepresented by both its critics and its proponents. We live at a pivotal moment in Church history. Like those men and women after the ecumenical councils of the past, we are now entrusted with ensuring the right implementation of Vatican II. How we respond to our task will impact the lives of generations to come. What we do with Vatican II will set the course for the Church in the third millennium.

This is a serious responsibility. But I hope you also see it as an exciting opportunity. My prayer is that this book has helped you see the Second Vatican Council in a new light, namely, in the light of the documents it generated. The council was not a liberal or conservative movement. It transcends today's political categories and cannot be genuinely interpreted through the opinions of mass media or worldly ideas. The council was inspired by the Holy Spirit and guided by his grace. It is the continuation of a long tradition in the Church. And it is the renewal of the Church's engagement with that tradition and its evangelistic posture toward the world.

Catholicism is not a stagnant institution. It is a living organism, dynamic and always developing. Through the centuries, the Church is in a constant process of reflecting on her salvation over and over again, always seeking new ways to share the timeless truths entrusted to her. What took place at Vatican II was the will of God. So as we look at the fallout of the post-conciliar decades, extending even to the present, we must not question whether the council was valid. We must rather question how the council's application went awry, and what we can do to reclaim it.

To that point, we learned about the paracouncil and how it manifested itself in three ways: the council of the theologians, the council of the media, and the council of the age. Those associated with the paracouncil saw in the flux and transition of Vatican II an opportunity to promote their own ideologies. And after a while, their assertions about the council became, for many Catholics, synonymous with the council itself. Universities, seminaries, and Catholic schools pushed the paracouncil's narrative to generations of laity, religious, and clergy. Most people did not even realize they were promoting paraconciliar ideas, believing their positions to be in sync with "the spirit of Vatican II."

The fallout included the rise of a reactionary form of traditionalism. Some Catholics came to associate the ideologies of the paracouncil with Vatican II itself and rejected the council, seeking refuge in pre-conciliar rituals and teachings. Nowhere is this reaction more pronounced than in the sacred liturgy, which remains the key point of contention between the paracouncil and traditionalists. Many of those who ascribe to traditionalism do so for good reasons: a love for beauty and sacredness in the liturgy, a commitment to orthodox catechesis and preaching, and a desire for a deeper sense of Catholic identity. But in the turn to traditionalism, this group misses out on the riches available in the Second Vatican Council—and finds itself in needless tension with a Church hierarchy that rightly seeks to promote Vatican II's legacy.

Vatican II's true intentions are often obscured and thwarted by these two extremes. At this point, outside of the polarized extremes, conversation about the council among typical practicing Catholics is basically extinct. Vatican II is simply not on most people's spiritual radar. But it should be.

Although the purpose of this book is to reflect on the spiritual foundations of the council and clarify points of misinterpretation, it is important to recognize that there were many things done right after Vatican II. In particular, the Church has made great strides in the arenas of evangelization, media outreach, social justice, ecumenism, scripture study, and pastoral accompaniment. That being said, there is still room for growth and reflection, especially in the sacred liturgy and catechesis.

So what now? How can we reclaim Vatican II? Let's turn to one of the founding bishops of the United States for our answer.

On August 15, 1790, Bishop John Carroll was ordained the first bishop of the United States. It was a long-fought battle convincing Rome to give America a bishop, but Carroll stuck to it. Just fourteen years after the Declaration of Independence, Carroll was entrusted with evangelizing one of the newest nations on earth. His job was not an easy one. The Church in the United States lacked resources and the faithful were uncatechized. On top of that, Carroll was the only Catholic prelate in a Protestant country. How was he to establish and renovate the faith in this land? Like many of the missionary bishops who had gone before him, Carroll knew that the answer to securing Catholic faith in America depended on two things: *piety* and *education*.

"Carroll's extant sermons, his diocesan synod of 1791 and his letters and instructions to his clergy stress the need for a general renewal of American Catholic piety . . . namely, the restoration of traditional Catholic practices, especially the frequent celebration of the Eucharist and Penance and a conversion of the heart that was essential for a fruitful reception of the Sacraments."[1] Sacred liturgy is always the basis of true reform. It is the premier activity of the Church and the source of her holiness. Reclaiming the

Church's liturgy from the paracouncil is step one. And this begins with the sacraments and the intentional restoration of beauty in accord with tradition.

Ars Celebrandi: It Starts with the Priest

Something that can lead to immediate positive change is priests remembering the *ars celebrandi*, "the art of celebration." This is a lot more than just the practical way we celebrate the liturgy. It refers to our whole attitude and demeanor toward our ministry. Even if he celebrates Mass in a barn, a good priest who prayerfully, obediently, and joyfully celebrates the sacraments can save souls. This demands that he be a man of prayer and devotion, especially to the Holy Eucharist. The Mass must be his lifeblood and the center of his universe. Everything else that takes place in the parish flows from the Mass.

When I was newly ordained, my bishop told me that a priest's first assignment is among the most influential in his ministry. He was not wrong. I learned things at St. Mary I will never forget. One of the most important lessons was the direct connection between my personal holiness and the holiness of the flock. My own passion, zeal, and commitment to the Church immediately spilled over into the hearts of my people. There is an old adage that claims, "A parish takes on the personality of its pastor." So true.

It was a shock to see how intimately tied I was to the people. We shared in a special communion that I did not know was possible. But, on further reflection, it made perfect sense. I am conformed to Christ through ordination. That makes the Church my bride, "and the two shall become one flesh" (Gn 2:24; Mt 19:5; Eph 5:31). I am sacramentally bound to my parish as a husband is to his wife. Do not the thoughts, feelings, and desires of a couple influence one another? Then why should it be any different for a parish priest and his flock?

So often we attempt to renew our parishes by subscribing to programs, buying new technologies, inviting in guest speakers, or doing retreats. These are good things and certainly to be encouraged. But they can never replace or surpass the day-in-and-day-out ministry of a parish priest. Bishop Carroll recognized this fact in the early days of our country. It is no different now. Celebrating the Mass with solemnity, devotion, and love—that alone will revolutionize the spirituality of a parish community. Couple that with heartfelt and joyful practice of the other sacraments, and you have the recipe for success.

I know some of my brother priests get weary of their ministry. Some even come to resent it. This is a temptation for all of us. The daily grind of parish life can be exhausting. Yet, we fall only when we lose sight of how awesome it is to be a priest. One of the primary ways Satan tempts priests is by making us forget the initial joy of our vocation—the expectation of ordination day, the happiness that filled our being when the bishop laid hands on our head, the humbling feeling of hearing our first Confession, the amazement at holding a newly baptized child, the heartbreak of burying a soul we anointed several days earlier. I think of those powerful words written by an anonymous poet:

> We need them in life's early morning,
> We need them again at its close;
> We feel their warm clasp of true friendship,
> We seek them when tasting life's woes.
> At the altar each day we behold them,
> And the hands of a king on his throne
> Are not equal to them in their greatness;
> Their dignity stands all alone;
> And when we are tempted and wander,
> To pathways of shame and of sin,
> It's the hand of a priest that will absolve us—
> Not once, but again and again.
> And when we are taking life's partner,

Other hands may prepare us a feast,
But the hand that will bless and unite us—
Is the beautiful hand of a priest.
God bless them and keep them all holy,
For the Host which their fingers caress;
When can a poor sinner do better,
Than to ask Him to guide thee and bless?
When the hour of death comes upon us,
May our courage and strength be increased,
By seeing raised over us in blessing—
The beautiful hands of a priest.

May we priests never forget the sheer beauty of our vocation. May we never underestimate its efficacy. The very life of our parishes depends on it. Trust in the sacraments. There is no greater gift God has left us. Jesus gave everything we need for vibrant faith communities. All we need to do is pour all our energy and resources into ensuring the beauty and solemnity of the liturgy.

Don't Underestimate the Power of Small, Intentional Steps

In addition to the *ars celebrandi*, the gradual reintegration of certain traditions will prove vital. This is especially important in the realm of sacred music, sacred art, sacred vessels, and architecture. The liturgical apostolate is also key—explaining the reasons behind certain practices and traditions, hosting regular evenings of reflection on Church history, theology, patristics, Latin, the lives of the saints, and so forth. People love that kind of stuff, especially if it is presented with enthusiasm and joy!

For my first parish assignment, I was sent to a community wounded by scandal and flailing in the spiritual life. After nearly two decades of lackluster parish life, they had received a new pastor. Thankfully, he was a holy priest working hard to renew hope and trust in people's hearts. When he arrived at the parish, school enrollment was down, finances were spiraling out of control, and the number of parishioners attending weekend Mass had dropped by more than 66 percent. On top of that, the church building was not the prettiest . . . and we will just leave it at that. I arrived as the pastor was in the middle of turning things around and immediately jumped on board to aid him in reviving the parish. Initially, everything was stacked against us. What could a priest do against such overwhelming circumstances?

In preparing for my first holy hour at the parish, I asked the Lord to help me know how to serve the people of St. Mary. His response was simple, but no less powerful for its simplicity: "Celebrate Mass with devotion and hear Confessions with love."

Be a priest and love the Church. That is all I had to do. So I set myself to celebrate every single Mass with utmost care. I poured my mind, heart, body, and soul into every word and every rubric. I trusted the liturgy. And it worked. After prioritizing the liturgy, we started slowly catechizing the people about the history of the Church, offering regular parish missions, and increasing the opportunities to celebrate the sacraments.

I'd like to take a moment to talk specifically to my fellow priests about what to expect in this process. Patience is essential. No one can turn a parish around immediately, and it is not pastoral to attempt to do so. The average parish takes three to five years to reform. The first three years are what I call the "catechetical stage." This is when we describe and form the people's hearts in light of the Church's teachings through the liturgy and extracurricular activities such as parish missions and retreats. Then, we start implementing changes over the next two years.

Before introducing any new liturgical practice, make sure to spend several weeks of catechesis with the people. Maybe you can have a "liturgical minute" before weekend Masses where different staff members go up to the ambo briefly before Mass to give short teachings on the liturgy. They can quote Church documents and explain the origins of various practices in the Mass. I have seen this implemented in several parishes to great effect. The community always appreciates it. The laity are understanding. We just need to explain things and give them the reason behind the Church's traditions. This is especially true among millennials and Gen Z Catholics, many of whom remain unaware of even the most basic aspects of our faith.

Something that was very important for our own parish was a well-formed and educated liturgical committee. Before we allowed the members to start suggesting or implementing any changes in the liturgy, we spent a whole year studying Church documents and texts on the liturgy. I assigned readings and study questions, and we met once a month to discuss them. Starting with *Sacrosanctum Concilium*, we talked about the ideals of Vatican II for the liturgy and how we could properly implement them in our parish.

Forming a community according to the ideals of Vatican II will take time. It needs to be prefaced by solid catechesis and a spirit of pastoral accompaniment. This is where some clergy and lay leaders have gotten into trouble. They arrive at a parish or a diocese that is in desperate need of reform, but they change things too abruptly and without due process. This leaves a bad taste in the mouths of the faithful. Conversion is a process and one that requires long-suffering. But if we stick with it and remain humble, the people will follow.

As I write this book, St. Mary Catholic Church and School are thriving. Our finances are in order, the school is filled with children, and Mass attendance is steadily increasing. Many of our new parishioners are young families. If you were to ask any of them why they are at St. Mary's they will give the same answer: "the liturgy and spirituality." People do not come to church to be entertained; they come to be sanctified. They desire an encounter with a holy God and expect to find it at Mass and in other liturgies.

Restoring the goodness of piety is the necessary first movement in reclaiming Vatican II.

As the people are exposed more and more to the beauty of sacred liturgy and the other sacraments, their identity as the Church is strengthened. They understand themselves as beloved children of God and see themselves as members of a pilgrim Church. This in turn inspires them to dive deeper into their faith. That leads us to the central importance of *education*.

Be Committed to Teaching and Learning–and Evangelizing

We know that Vatican II was inspired by the Church Fathers and sacred scripture as well as driven by a missionary impulse to sanctify the world. This falls perfectly in sync with the need for education. The first thing we must do is educate ourselves through the study of scripture and reading the Church Fathers. No generation of Catholics in history has had more resources for Bible study than we do. Add to that the unbelievable fact that so many writings of the Church Fathers are freely available in English and other languages, and we can only conclude that this is a great time to be a Catholic. A world of resources in the form of books, free websites, and apps—utterly unimaginable to previous generations—is literally at our fingertips.

As good as private study is, it is always better in a group. Parishes can host study and reading groups focused on the Church Fathers. The bulletin is a good place to publish writings and reflections about the Church Fathers and scripture. Also, one of the main purposes of this book is to encourage you to read Vatican II! We can't reclaim Vatican II if we haven't read the documents. Simply spending time firsthand with the documents of Vatican II, especially the four major constitutions covered in this book, is imperative if we hope to reclaim the council. It would bear amazing fruit in the Church if the laity were well-read in the teachings of the council. We are fortunate to have all of the documents in the vernacular, readily accessible on the Vatican website.

Although this book provides an introduction to and background for the current state of Vatican II's implementation in the Church and identifies the urgent need to reclaim the council, we were not able to go into extensive detail about each of the documents. There are a number of excellent books that can aid in further study of Vatican II and its documents.

For general and easily readable information on Vatican II, Aidan Nichols's *Conciliar Octet: A Concise Commentary on the Eight Key Texts of the Second Vatican Council* is top-notch. It provides a brief overview of the four major documents as well as four other important minor documents. *What Went Wrong with Vatican II: The Catholic Crisis Explained*, by Ralph M. McInerny, is another good read. Although he does not speak directly about the paracouncil, McInerny does touch on some of the major issues after Vatican II that have brought so much tension to the Church. For a more academic work, look into *Vatican II: Renewal within Tradition*, edited by Matthew L. Lamb and Matthew Levering. This book is worth purchasing simply for the introduction by Pope Benedict XVI, in which he explains the hermeneutic of rupture versus the hermeneutic of continuity. In reference to the liturgy, I strongly recommend *The Spirit of the Liturgy*, also by Benedict XVI (written when he was Cardinal Joseph Ratzinger). No other book better explains Vatican II's vision for the liturgy. It also gives profound theological insights about different aspects of the liturgy and provides practical advice for how the Church can grow in her devotions.

Finally, after educating ourselves and being formed by the holiness of Mother Church, we need to evangelize. The Second Vatican Council sought to open the doors of the Church—not so that the Church could become more worldly, but so that the world could become more holy. Each of us receives the call to be a missionary evangelist at the moment of our baptism. Throughout our lives, Christ calls us anew every day to follow him and preach the Gospel. As Pope Francis reminds us,

> The joy of the gospel fills the hearts and lives of all who encounter Jesus. Those who accept his offer of salvation are set free from sin, sorrow, inner emptiness and loneliness. With Christ joy is constantly born anew. In this Exhortation I wish to encourage the Christian faithful to embark upon a new chapter of evangelization marked by this joy.[2]

•••

We find ourselves at a crucial moment in Church history. It is not an accident that you are alive here and now. Nor is it a coincidence that you are reading this book. You and I were both made for this moment. For some reason that we will only fully understand in heaven, God has seen something in you, special gifts and talents that he knows are perfect for the situation in which we find ourselves as Catholics. We do not have to waste time trying to figure out our task. The Holy Spirit gave it to us plainly in the Second Vatican Council. All we need to do now is reclaim it.

NOTES

Foreword

1. John Cavadini, "Was Vatican II a Bad Seed?" *Church Life Journal*, July 29, 2020, https://churchlifejournal.nd.edu/articles/is-vatican-ii-bad-seed/; John Cavadini, "Co-Responsibility: An Antidote to Clericalizing the Laity?" *Church Life Journal*, March 26, 2020, https://churchlifejournal.nd.edu/articles/co-responsibility-is-the-remedy-for-lay-clericalism/.

Introduction

1. Henri de Lubac, *A Brief Catechesis on Nature and Grace*, trans. Richard Arnandez (San Francisco: Ignatius Press, 1984), 235–38.

2. de Lubac, *A Brief Catechesis*, 236.

3. Joseph Ratzinger with Vittorio Messori, *The Ratzinger Report: An Exclusive Interview on the State of the Church*, trans. Salvator Attanasio and Graham Harrison (San Francisco: Ignatius Press, 1985), 31.

4. Robert Barron, *Bridging the Great Divide: Musings of a Post-Liberal, Post-Conservative, Evangelical Catholic* (Lanham, MD: Rowman & Littlefield, 2004), xi.

5. Ratzinger with Messori, *The Ratzinger Report*, 40.

1. The Paracouncil: What Happened?

1. Joseph Ratzinger, *The Nature and Mission of Theology: Essays to Orient Theology in Today's Debates*, trans. Adrian Walker (San Francisco: Ignatius Press, 1995), 102.

2. Pope Benedict XVI, quoted in Matthew L. Lamb and Matthew Levering, eds., *Vatican II: Renewal within Tradition* (Oxford: Oxford University Press, 2008), x.

3. Henri de Lubac, *The Motherhood of the Church*, trans. Sergia Englund (San Francisco: Ignatius Press, 1982), 25–27. Emphasis added.

4. Congregation for the Doctrine of the Faith, *Donum Veritatis: On the Ecclesial Vocation of the Theologian* (1990), Vatican Archive, http://www.vatican.va/roman_curia/congregations/cfaith/documents/rc_con_cfaith_doc_19900524_theologian-vocation_en.html, 22. Emphasis added.

5. Edward Schillebeeckx, *Approches théologiques* (Brussels: Éditions de C.E.P., 1967), vol. 3, ch. 2, sec. 1, pt. 3, "L'Église sacrament du monde," as read in de Lubac, *A Brief Catechesis*, 191.

6. Benedict XVI, "The Church and the Scandal of Sexual Abuse," *Catholic News Agency*, April 10, 2019, https://www.catholicnewsagency.com/news/full-text-of-benedict-xvi-the-church-and-the-scandal-of-sexual-abuse-59639.

7. Lamb and Levering, *Vatican II*, 3.

8. "Pope Shares with U.S. Bishops His Frustration with Reaction to Amazon Text," *Crux* (February 13, 2020), https://cruxnow.com/vatican/2020/02/pope-shares-with-u-s-bishops-his-frustration-with-reaction-to-amazon-text/.

9. Clement I, "Who Can Express the Binding Power of Divine Love?" *Liturgy of the Hours*, Volume III, pg. 88.

10. William Shakespeare, *Love's Labour's Lost*, Act IV, Scene II.

11. Aidan Nichols, *Conciliar Octet: A Concise Commentary on the Eight Key Texts of the Second Vatican Council* (San Francisco: Ignatius Press, 2019), 17–18.

12. Bernard Tissier de Mallerais, *Marcel Lefebvre: The Biography*, trans. Brian Sudlow (Kansas City, MO: Angelus Press, 2004), 430.

13. "The Heart of the SSPX: The Catholic Priesthood and the Integrity of the Faith," SSPX website, https://sspx.org/en/about.

14. John Paul II, *Vicesimus Quintus Annus* (1988), Vatican Archive, http://www.vatican.va/content/john-paul-ii/en/apost_letters/1988/documents/hf_jp-ii_apl_19881204_vicesimus-quintus-annus.html, 11–13.

15. "The Sermon of His Excellency Archbishop Marcel Lefebvre," June 30, 1988, Society of St. Pius—District of Asia, https://www.sspxasia.com/Documents/Archbishop-Lefebvre/Episcopal-Consecration.htm.

16. Moyra Doorly and Aidan Nichols, *The Council in Question: A Dialogue with Catholic Traditionalism* (Charlotte, NC: Tan Books, 2013), 3–4.

17. Pope Francis, *Evangelii Gaudium* (Washington, DC: USCCB, 2013).

2. The True Spirit of Vatican II

1. Vincent of Lérins, *Commonitory*, in *The Church Fathers*, ed. Philip Schaff and Henry Wace, vol. 11 of *Nicene and Post-Nicene Fathers*, sec. ser. (Peabody, MA: Hendrickson Publishers, 2012), 135.

2. Vincent of Lérins, *Commonitory*, 134.

3. Vincent of Lérins, *Commonitory*, 147–48.

4. Joseph Ratzinger, *Introduction to Christianity*, trans. J. R. Foster (San Francisco: Communio Books, 2004), 96.

5. Nicholas J. Healy Jr., and Matthew Levering, eds., *Ressourcement after Vatican II: Essays in Honor of Joseph Fessio, S.J.* (San Francisco, CA: Ignatius Press, 2019), 357.

6. Robert P. Imbelli, *Rekindling the Christic Imagination* (Collegeville, MN: Liturgical Press, 2014), xiii–xiv.

7. Augustine of Hippo, "Exposition on the Psalms," in *The Church Fathers*, ed. Philip Schaff and Henry Wace, vol. 11 of *Nicene and Post-Nicene Fathers*, sec. ser. (Peabody, MA: Hendrickson Publishers, 2012), 135.

8. Augustine of Hippo, "Exposition on the Psalms," 167.

9. G. K. Chesterton, *Orthodoxy*, 2nd ed. (Des Plaines, IL: Word on Fire, 2018), 43.

10. Yves Congar, *The Meaning of Tradition*, trans. A. N. Woodrow (San Francisco: Ignatius Press, 2004), 10.

11. John Paul II, *Ecclesia de Eucharistia* (2003), Vatican Archive, http://www.vatican.va/holy_father/special_features/encyclicals/documents/hf_jp-ii_enc_20030417_eccle, 49.

12. Imbelli, *Rekindling the Christic Imagination*, xv.

3. The Sacred Liturgy

1. Benedict of Nursia, *Rule of St. Benedict* (Order of St. Benedict), XLII, http://archive.osb.org/rb/text/rbemjo2.html#43.

2. See Pius X, *Tra Le Sollecitudini,* and Pius XII, *Maxima Redemptionis.*

3. Melito of Sardis, *On Pascha,* trans. Alistair C. Stewart (Yonkers, NY: St. Vladimir's Seminary Press, 2016), 63.

4. Ephrem the Syrian, *Hymns on Paradise*, trans. Sebastian Brock (Crestwood, NY: St. Vladimir's Seminary Press, 1990), 99.

5. Gregory of Nyssa, in *Ancient Christian Commentary on Scripture. Old Testament I: Genesis 1–11,* ed. Andrew Louth (Downers Grove, IL: InterVarsity Press, 2001), 78.

6. Symeon the New Theologian, *On the Mystical Life: The Ethical Discourses*, trans. Alexander Golitzin (Crestwood, NY: St. Vladimir's Seminary Press, 1995), 32.

7. Joseph Raya, *Acathist Hymn: Office of Praise to the Name of Jesus*, ed. Austin Flannery (Combermere, ON, Canada: Madonna House Publications, 2016), 9.

8. *Roman Missal,* Eucharistic Prayer III (Totowa, NJ: Catholic Book Publishing Corp., 2011), 505.

9. Severian of Gabala, in *Ancient Christian Commentary on Scripture. Old Testament I,* 60.

10. Albert Vanhoye, *Christ Our High Priest*, ed. Austin Flannery (Australia: Modotti Press, 2010), 92.

11. Joseph Ratzinger, *The Spirit of the Liturgy* (2000; San Francisco: Ignatius Press, 2018), 185.

12. Guido Marini, *Liturgical Reflections of a Papal Master of Ceremonies*, trans. Nicholas L. Gregoris (Pine Beach, NJ: Newman House Press, 2011), 24.

13. Ratzinger, *Spirit of the Liturgy*, 187.

14. Marini, *Liturgical Reflections*, 24.

15. *General Instruction of the Roman Missal* 45.

16. Commission on the Sacred Liturgy, *Inter Oecumenici: Instruction on Implementing Liturgical Norms*, 1964, 91, Adoremus, https://adoremus.org/1964/09/inter-oecumenici/.

17. Basil the Great, in *Ancient Christian Commentary on Scripture. Old Testament I*, 54.

18. Germanus of Constantinople, *On the Divine Liturgy*, trans. Paul Meyendorff (New York: St. Vladimir's Seminary Press, 1984), 65.

19. Ratzinger, *Spirit of the Liturgy*, 91.

20. Fr. Louis Boyer, as read in Ratzinger, *Spirit of the Liturgy*, 92.

21. Ratzinger, *Spirit of the Liturgy*, 91.

22. Ratzinger, *Spirit of the Liturgy*, 94.

23. Ratzinger, *Spirit of the Liturgy*, 83–84.

24. Paul VI, *Jubilate Deo* (Musica Sacra Forum, 2018), https://forum.musicasacra.com/forum/discussion/16016/jubilate-deo-booklet/p1.

25. John Paul II, *Vicesimus Quintus Annus*, 10.

26. Benedict XVI, *Summorum Pontificum* (2007), Vatican Archive, http://www.vatican.va/content/benedict-xvi/en/motu_proprio/documents/hf_ben-xvi_motu-proprio_20070707_summorum-pontificum.html. While Pope Francis's July 16, 2021 motu proprio, Traditionis Custodes, limits the celebration of the extraordinary form of the Mass (celebrated in Latin) that Summorum Pontificum had allowed, Francis identifies this limitation as a "burden" for the sake of unity in his accompanying letter to bishops

around the world. https://press.vatican.va/content/salastampa/it/bollettino/pubblico/2021/07/16/0469/01015.html#ingL

27. Pope Francis, *Evangelii Gaudium*, 135–36.

28. General Instruction of the Liturgy of the Hours, Vol. I of the *Liturgy of the Hours*, 27.

29. Ibid.

30. Fulton J. Sheen, *The Priest Is Not His Own* (San Francisco: Ignatius Press, 1963), 73.

31. Columba Marmion, *Christ, the Ideal of the Priest* (San Francisco: Ignatius Press, 1952), 73.

32. Marmion, *Christ, the Ideal of the Priest*, 73.

33. Elizabeth Lev, *How Catholic Art Saved the Faith: The Triumph of Beauty and Truth in Counter-Reformation Art* (Manchester, NH: Sophia Institute Press, 2018), 19.

34. Denis McNamara, *Catholic Church Architecture and the Spirit of the Liturgy* (Chicago: Hillenbrand Books, 2009), 1.

35. McNamara, *Catholic Church Architecture*, 5.

36. Blake Britton, "Video Games: A Lesson on the Importance of Aesthetics," *Word on Fire*, May 2019, https://www.wordonfire.org/resources/blog/video-games-a-lesson-on-the-importance-of-aesthetics/23928/.

37. *Code of Canon Law*, 1254 §2.

4. The Church

1. John R. Donahue and Daniel J. Harrington, *The Gospel of Mark* (Collegeville, MN: Liturgical Press, 2002), 71.

2. Johann Adam Möhler, *Unity in the Church, or The Principle of Catholicism: Presented in the Spirit of the Church Fathers of the First Three Centuries*, ed. and trans. Peter C. Erb (Washington, DC: Catholic University of America Press, 1996), 94.

3. Joseph Ratzinger, *Pilgrim Fellowship of Faith: The Church as Communion*, trans. Henry Taylor (San Francisco: Ignatius Press, 2005), 42.

4. Cyprian of Carthage, *On the Church: Select Treatises*, trans. Allen Brent (Crestwood, NY: St. Vladimir's Seminary Press, 2006), 110.

5. John Paul II, *Ecclesia de Eucharistia*, 44.

6. Nichols, *Conciliar Octet*, 48.

7. *Roman Missal*, The Passion of the Lord, 187.

8. John Chrysostom, as read in the *Liturgy of the Hours*, Volume II: Hours, Good Friday, Office of Readings.

9. John Paul II, *Christifideles Laici* (1988), Vatican Archive, http://www.vatican.va/content/john-paul-ii/en/apost_exhortations/documents/hf_jp-ii_exh_30121988_christifideles-laici.html, 15. Emphasis in the original.

10. Josemaría Escrivá, "The Message of Opus Dei," *Opus Dei*, https://opusdei.org/en-us/article/message/.

11. Thérèse of Lisieux, "In the Heart of the Church I Will Be Love," Office of Readings for October 2, *Liturgy of the Hours*, Volume IV.

12. *Roman Missal*, Eucharistic Prayer for Use in Masses for Various Need II, 631.

13. John of Damascus, *Wider Than Heaven: Eighth-Century Homilies on the Mother of God*, trans. Mary B. Cunningham (Crestwood, NY: St. Vladimir's Seminary Press, 2008), 62.

14. Bernard of Clairvaux, "In Praise of the Virgin Mother," Office of Readings for December 20, *Liturgy of the Hours*, Volume I.

15. Joseph Cardinal Ratzinger and Hans Urs von Balthasar, *Mary, the Church at the Source*, trans. Adrian Walker (San Francisco: Ignatius Press, 2005), 110.

16. *Roman Missal*, Masses of the Blessed Virgin Mary (Totowa, NJ: Catholic Book Publishing Corp., 2012), 124.

5. Divine Revelation

1. Gregory of Nazianzus, *On God and Man*, trans. Peter Gilbert (Crestwood, NY: St. Vladimir's Seminary Press, 2001), 39.

2. Augustine, *On the Gospel of John* (Peabody, MA: Hendrickson Publishers, 1994), 13.

3. Maximus the Confessor, *On the Cosmic Mystery of Jesus Christ*, trans. Paul M. Blowers and Robert Louis Wilken (Crestwood, NY: St. Vladimir's Seminary Press, 2003), 125.

4. John Paul II, *Redemptor Hominis* (Boston: Pauline Press, 1979), 1.

5. Hans Urs von Balthasar, *The Glory of the Lord*, vol. 1: *Seeing the Form*, trans. Erasmo Leiva-Merikakis (San Francisco: Ignatius Press, 2009), 30.

6. Jerome, "Ignorance of Scripture Is Ignorance of Christ," Office of Readings for September 30, *Liturgy of the Hours*, Volume IV.

7. Balthasar, *Glory of the Lord*, vol. 1, 31.

8. See Albert Schweitzer, *The Quest of the Historical Jesus*, chap. 3, "The Lives of Jesus of the Earlier Rationalism."

9. Luke Timothy Johnson, *The Gospel of Luke* (Collegeville, MN: Liturgical Press, 1991), 143.

10. Benedict XVI, *Jesus of Nazareth, Part Two: Holy Week. From the Entrance into Jerusalem to the Resurrection* (San Francisco. Ignatius Press, 2011), xiv–xv.

11. Benedict XVI, *Jesus of Nazareth, Part Two: Holy Week*, xv.

6. The Church and the Modern World

1. Joseph Ratzinger, *Christianity and the Crisis of Culture*, trans. Brian McNeil (San Francisco: Ignatius Press, 2006), 26.

2. Joseph Ratzinger, *Theological Highlights of Vatican II* (New York: Paulist Press, 2009), 232.

3. Erin McDowell, "13 Surprising Facts about Divorce in the US," July 3, 2020, https://www.businessinsider.com/alarming-facts-about-divorce-in-the-us.

4. GLAAD, *Where We Are on TV Report, 2019–2020*, https://www.glaad.org/whereweareontv19, p. 9.

5. John Paul II, *Man and Woman He Created Them: A Theology of the Body*, trans. Michael M. Waldstein (Boston: Pauline Books & Media, 2006), 3:1.

6. John Paul II, *Man and Woman He Created Them*, 5:6.

7. Paul VI, *Humanae Vitae* (1968), Vatican Archive, http://www.vatican.va/content/paul-vi/en/encyclicals/documents/hf_p-vi_enc_25071968_humanae-vitae.ht, 17.

7. What Now?

1. Patrick W. Carey, *Catholics in America: A History* (New York: Rowman & Littlefield, 2004), 18.

2. Pope Francis, *Evangelii Gaudium*, 1.

BIBLIOGRAPHY

Ancient Christian Commentary on Scripture. Old Testament I: Genesis 1–11, edited by Andrew Louth. Downers Grove, IL: InterVarsity Press, 2001.

Augustine of Hippo. *Confessions*. Des Plaines, IL: Word on Fire, 2017.

———. "Exposition on the Psalms." In *The Church Fathers*, edited by Philip Schaff and Henry Wace. Vol. 11 of *Nicene and Post-Nicene Fathers*. Sec. ser. Peabody, MA: Hendrickson Publishers, 2012, 135.

———. *On the Gospel of John*. Peabody, MA: Hendrickson Publishers, 1994.

Balthasar, Hans Urs von. *Seeing the Form*. Vol. 1 of *The Glory of the Lord*. Translated by Erasmo Leiva-Merikakis. San Francisco: Ignatius Press, 2009.

Barron, Robert. *Bridging the Great Divide: Musings of a Post-Liberal, Post-Conservative, Evangelical Catholic*. Lanham, MD: Rowman & Littlefield, 2004.

Benedict of Nursia. *Rule of St. Benedict*. Order of St. Benedict. http://archive.osb.org/rb/text/rbemjo2.html#43.

Benedict XVI. "The Church and the Scandal of Sexual Abuse." *Catholic News Agency*, April 10, 2019. https://www.catholicnewsagency.com/news/full-text-of-benedict-xvi-the-church-and-the-scandal-of-sexual-abuse-59639.

————. *Jesus of Nazareth, Part Two: Holy Week. From the Entrance into Jerusalem to the Resurrection.* San Francisco: Ignatius Press, 2011.

————. *Summorum Pontificum.* 2007. Vatican Archive, http://www.vatican.va/content/benedict-xvi/en/motu_proprio/documents/hf_ben-xvi_motu-proprio_20070707_summorum-pontificum.html.

————. *See also* Ratzinger, Joseph.

Bergsma, John, and Brant Pitre. *A Catholic Introduction to the Bible: The Old Testament.* San Francisco: Ignatius Press, 2018.

Carey, Patrick W. *Catholics in America: A History.* New York: Rowman & Littlefield, 2004.

Chesterton, G. K. *Orthodoxy.* 2nd ed. Des Plaines, IL: Word on Fire, 2018.

Commission on the Sacred Liturgy. *Inter Oecumenici: Instruction on Implementing Liturgical Norms.* 1964. Adoremus, https://adoremus.org/1964/09/inter-oecumenici/.

Congar, Yves. *The Meaning of Tradition.* Translated by A. N. Woodrow. San Francisco: Ignatius Press, 2004.

Congregation for the Doctrine of the Faith. *Donum Veritatis: On the Ecclesial Vocation of the Theologian.* 1990. Vatican Archive, http://www.vatican.va/roman_curia/congregations/cfaith/documents/rc_con_cfaith_doc_19900524_theologian-vocation_en.html.

Cyprian of Carthage. *On the Church: Select Treatises.* Translated by Allen Brent. Crestwood, NY: St. Vladimir's Seminary Press, 2006.

De Lubac, Henri. *A Brief Catechesis on Nature and Grace.* Translated by Richard Arnandez. San Francisco: Ignatius Press, 1984.

————. *Catholicism: Christ and the Common Destiny of Man.* Translated by Lancelot C. Sheppard and Elizabeth Englund. San Francisco: Ignatius Press, 1988.

————. *The Motherhood of the Church*. Translated by Sergia Englund. San Francisco: Ignatius Press, 1982.

Donahue, John R., and Daniel J. Harrington. *The Gospel of Mark*. Collegeville, MN: Liturgical Press, 2002.

Doorly, Moyra, and Aidan Nichols. *The Council in Question: A Dialogue with Catholic Traditionalism*. Charlotte, NC: Tan Books, 2013.

Ephrem the Syrian. *Hymns on Paradise*. Translated by Sebastian Brock. Crestwood, NY: St. Vladimir's Seminary Press, 1990.

Escrivá, Josemaría. "The Message of Opus Dei." *Opus Dei*, https://opusdei.org/en-us/article/message/.

Francis. *Evangelii Gaudium*. Washington, DC: USCCB, 2013.

————. "Letter of the Holy Father Francis to the Bishops of the Whole World, that Accompanies the Apostolic Letter Motu Proprio Traditionis Custodes." 2021. https://press.vatican.va/content/salastampa/it/bollettino/pubblico/2021/07/16/0469/01015.html#ingL

Germanus of Constantinople. *On the Divine Liturgy*. Translated by Paul Meyendorff. Crestwood, NY: St. Vladimir's Seminary Press, 1984.

GLAAD. *Where We Are on TV Report, 2019–2020*. https://www.glaad.org/whereweareontv19.

Gregory of Nazianzus. *On God and Man*. Translated by Peter Gilbert. Crestwood, NY: St. Vladimir's Seminary Press, 2001.

Healy, Nicholas J., Jr. "The Spirit of Christian Doctrine." *Communio International Catholic Review* 43, no. 2 (Summer 2016): 239.

Healy, Nicholas J., Jr., and Matthew Levering, eds. *Ressourcement after Vatican II: Essays in Honor of Joseph Fessio, S.J.* San Francisco: Ignatius Press, 2019.

Imbelli, Robert P. *Rekindling the Christic Imagination*. Collegeville, MN: Liturgical Press, 2014.

John of Damascus. *Wider Than Heaven: Eighth-Century Homilies on the Mother of God.* Translated by Mary B. Cunningham. Crestwood, NY: St. Vladimir's Seminary Press, 2008.

John Paul II. *Christifideles Laici.* 1988. Vatican Archive, http://www.vatican.va/content/john-paul-ii/en/apost_exhortations/documents/hf_jp-ii_exh_30121988_christifideles-laici.html.

———. *Ecclesia de Eucharistia.* 2003. Vatican Archive, http://www.vatican.va/holy_father/special_features/encyclicals/documents/hf_jp-ii_enc_20030417_ecclesia_eucharistia_en.html.

———. *Man and Woman He Created Them: A Theology of the Body.* Translated by Michael M. Waldstein. Boston: Pauline Books & Media, 2006.

———. *Redemptor Hominis.* Boston: Pauline Press, 1979.

———. *Vicesimus Quintus Annus.* 1988. Vatican Archive, http://www.vatican.va/content/john-paul-ii/en/apost_letters/1988/documents/hf_jp-ii_apl_19881204_vicesimus-quintus-annus.html.

Johnson, Luke Timothy. *The Gospel of Luke.* Collegeville, MN: Liturgical Press, 1991.

Lamb, Matthew L., and Matthew Levering, eds. *Vatican II: Renewal within Tradition.* Oxford: Oxford University Press, 2008.

Lev, Elizabeth. *How Catholic Art Saved the Faith: The Triumph of Beauty and Truth in Counter-Reformation Art.* Manchester, NH: Sophia Institute Press, 2018.

Marini, Guido. *Liturgical Reflections of a Papal Master of Ceremonies.* Translated by Nicholas L. Gregoris. Pine Beach, NJ: Newman House Press, 2011.

Marmion, Columba. *Christ, the Ideal of the Priest.* San Francisco: Ignatius Press, 1952.

Maximus the Confessor. *On the Cosmic Mystery of Jesus Christ.*
Translated by Paul M. Blowers and Robert Louis Wilken.
Crestwood, NY: St. Vladimir's Seminary Press, 2003.

McDowell, Erin. "13 Surprising Facts about Divorce in the
US." July 3, 2020. https://www.businessinsider.com/
alarming-facts-about-divorce-in-the-us.

McNamara, Denis. *Catholic Church Architecture and the Spirit of
the Liturgy.* Chicago: Hildebrand Books, 2009.

Melito of Sardis. *On Pascha.* Translated by Alistair C. Stewart.
Yonkers, NY: St. Vladimir's Seminary Press, 2016.

Möhler, Johann Adam. *Unity in the Church, or The Principle of
Catholicism: Presented in the Spirit of the Church Fathers
of the First Three Centuries.* Edited and translated by Peter
C. Erb. Washington, DC: Catholic University of America
Press, 1996.

Nichols, Aidan. *Conciliar Octet: A Concise Commentary on the
Eight Key Texts of the Second Vatican Council.* San Francisco: Ignatius Press, 2019.

Paul VI. *Humanae Vitae.* 1968. Vatican Archive, http://www.vat-
ican.va/content/paul-vi/en/encyclicals/documents/hf_p-
vi_enc_25071968_humanae-vitae.ht.

———. *Jubilate Deo.* Musica Sacra Forum, 2018, https://
forum.musicasacra.com/forum/discussion/16016/
jubilate-deo-booklet/p1.

Ratzinger, Joseph. *Christianity and the Crisis of Culture.* Translated
by Brian McNeil. San Francisco: Ignatius Press, 2006.

———. *"In the Beginning": A Catholic Understanding of the Story
of Creation and the Fall.* London: T&T Clark, 1995.

———. *Introduction to Christianity.* Translated by J. R. Foster. San
Francisco: Communio Books, 2004.

———. *The Nature and Mission of Theology: Essays to Orient Theology in Today's Debates.* Translated by Adrian Walker. San
Francisco: Ignatius Press, 1995.

————. *Pilgrim Fellowship of Faith: The Church as Communion*. Translated by Henry Taylor. San Francisco: Ignatius Press, 2005.

————. *The Spirit of the Liturgy*. 1999; San Francisco: Ignatius Press, 2018.

————. *Theological Highlights of Vatican II*. New York: Paulist Press, 2009.

————. *See also* Benedict XVI.

Ratzinger, Joseph Cardinal, and Hans Urs von Balthasar. *Mary, the Church at the Source*. Translated by Adrian Walker. San Francisco: Ignatius Press, 2005.

Ratzinger, Joseph, with Vittorio Messori. *The Ratzinger Report: An Exclusive Interview on the State of the Church*. Translated by Salvator Attanasio and Graham Harrison. San Francisco: Ignatius Press, 1985.

Raya, Joseph. *Acathist Hymn: Office of Praise to the Name of Jesus*. Edited by Austin Flannery. Combermere, ON, Canada: Madonna House Publications, 2016.

Roman Missal. Masses of the Blessed Virgin Mary. Totowa, NJ: Catholic Book Publishing Corp., 2012.

Schindler, D. C. "Perfect Difference: Gender and the Analogy of Being," *Communio: International Catholic Review* 43, no. 2 (Summer 2016): 228.

Sheen, Fulton J. *The Priest Is Not His Own*. San Francisco: Ignatius Press, 1963.

Symeon the New Theologian. *On the Mystical Life: The Ethical Discourses*. Translated by Alexander Golitzin. Crestwood, NY: St. Vladimir's Seminary Press, 1995.

Tissier de Mallerais, Bernard. *Marcel Lefebvre: The Biography*. Translated by Brian Sudlow. Kansas City, MO: Angelus Press, 2004.

Vanhoye, Albert. *Christ Our High Priest*. Edited by Austin Flannery. Australia: Modotti Press, 2010.

Vatican Council II. *The Conciliar and Post-Conciliar Documents.*
    Edited by Austin Flannery. New York: Costello Publishing
    Co., 2004.
Vincent of Lérins. *Commonitory.* In *The Church Fathers*, edited
    by Philip Schaff and Henry Wace. Vol. 11 of *Nicene and
    Post-Nicene Fathers.* Sec. ser. Peabody, MA: Hendrickson
    Publishers, 2012.

Fr. Blake Britton serves as a parish priest and assistant vocations director in the Diocese of Orlando. He is a regular contributor to the Word on Fire Institute's blog and its *Evangelization & Culture* journal. He also cohosts *The Burrowshire Podcast* with Brandon Vogt.

Britton earned his bachelor's degree in philosophy from St. John Vianney College-Seminary and his master's degree in divinity from St. Vincent de Paul Regional Seminary. He has contributed to two anthologies. He has appeared on EWTN, The Catholic Channel, and a number of radio programs and podcasts.

He is a classically trained opera singer, pianist, and organist and is trained in classical Latin and biblical Greek.

Facebook: Fr. Blake Britton
Instagram: Fr. Blake Britton
YouTube: The Burrowshire Podcast

John C. Cavadini is the McGrath-Cavadini director of the McGrath Institute for Church Life at the University of Notre Dame.

The Word on Fire
VATICAN II COLLECTION

A robust but readable journey into the true history and purpose of the Second Vatican Council, and a compelling call for an enthusiastic return to its texts today.

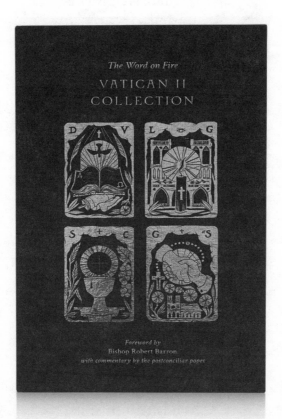

The *Word on Fire Vatican II Collection* features the four central documents that most fully articulate the vision of the council—*Dei Verbum, Lumen Gentium, Sacrosanctum Concilium*, and *Gaudium et Spes*—with illuminating commentary from the postconciliar popes and Bishop Robert Barron interspersed throughout, along with beautifully carved linocut art. The collection also includes the opening address of Pope St. John XXIII, the closing address of Pope St. Paul VI, a foreword from Bishop Barron, an afterword from theologian Matthew Levering, and helpful appendices listing key terms and figures and answering frequently asked questions.

Learn more and get your copy at **wordonfire.org/vatican2**.

AVE

AVE MARIA PRESS

Founded in 1865, Ave Maria Press,
a ministry of the Congregation of
Holy Cross, is a Catholic publishing
company that serves the spiritual and
formative needs of the Church and its
schools, institutions, and ministers;
Christian individuals and families; and
others seeking spiritual nourishment.

For a complete listing of titles from

Ave Maria Press

Sorin Books

Forest of Peace

Christian Classics

visit www.avemariapress.com

AVE | AVE MARIA PRESS
    | Notre Dame, IN
A Ministry of the United States Province of Holy Cross